CITYSPOTS

LISBO

Louise Pole-Baker

Written by Louise Pole-Baker
Updated by Anja Mutic

Published by Thomas Cook Publishing
A division of Thomas Cook Tour Operations Limited
Company registration No: 1450464 England
The Thomas Cook Business Park, 9 Coningsby Road
Peterborough PE3 8SB, United Kingdom
Email: books@thomascook.com, Tel: +44 (0)1733 416477
www.thomascookpublishing.com

Produced by The Content Works Ltd
Aston Court, Kingsmead Business Park, Frederick Place
High Wycombe, Bucks HP11 1LA
www.thecontentworks.com

Series design based on an original concept by Studio 183 Limited

ISBN: 978-1-84157- 966-5

Series Editor: Kelly Anne Pipes
Production/DTP: Steven Collins

Printed and bound in Spain by GraphyCems

CONTENTS

SYMBOLS KEY

The following symbols are used throughout this book:

ⓐ address ⓣ telephone ⓦ website address

opening times public transport connections

The following symbols are used on the maps:

i	information office	■	points of interest
✈	airport	O	city
✚	hospital	O	large town
	police station	○	small town
	bus station		motorway
	railway station	–	main road
Ⓜ	metro		minor road
✝	cathedral	–	railway

❶ numbers denote featured cafés & restaurants

Hotels and restaurants are graded by approximate price as follows:

£ budget price **££** mid-range price **£££** expensive

In addresses, 'Avenida' (meaning 'avenue') is abbreviated to 'Av.'

Rossio has been one of Lisbon's main squares since the Middle Ages

INTRODUCING Lisbon

Introduction

The Portuguese capital is a city on a human scale, and its immediately likeable atmosphere is the gateway to a rich cultural background. History and politics are inscribed on its soul and written into its unique geography. Get up high on the Elevador de Santa Justa and look out over the cobbled, hilly streets and hotchpotch of roofs and alleyways that cover Lisbon's seven hills. At one end of the city you'll see the Castelo de São Jorge, towering over an area that forms a powerful historical and architectural reminder of the city's reclamation from the Moors. At the other end of Lisbon, the 1960s Padrão dos Descobrimentos is a monument to its maritime glories. The 25 de Abril Bridge and the modern Vasco da Gama Bridge – the longest bridge in Europe – link their most famous maritime hero to the modern European city of today. The ruins of the Convento do Carmo date back to the devastating 1755 earthquake; the rebuilt, earthquake-proof Baixa area is testament to the city's successful reconstruction.

Decorative blue *azulejos* tiles cover palaces, houses and even metro stations, telling the fascinating story of Portugal's social and cultural history. Inside the palaces, the opulent décor harks back to the wealth squandered by the royal family and ruling classes before the rise of Portugal's former dictator Salazar. Large parts of Lisbon's architectural landscape have been transformed since Portugal's transition to democracy, from the contemporary building and walkways of the Centro Cultural de Belém to the ambitious Parque das Nações, where everything is named after heroes from the past. Lisbon's urban landscape continues to evolve as the country's economy strengthens.

Located at the mouth of the Rio Tejo (River Tagus), the city has a rich gastronomy influenced both by the sea and by its imperial history. In the streets you'll smell smoky, roasting chestnuts and freshly baked custard tarts, and in the restaurants they'll serve up salted cod or fresh sardines washed down with young *vinho verde* wine and fiery after-dinner *ginginha*.

Fado music and other sounds fill the air in the historic Bairro Alto. However you like to spend your days and evenings, immerse yourself in Lisbon's unique, enticing atmosphere and you're sure to find something to entertain you.

Vasco da Gama is the longest bridge in Europe with a total length of 17.2 km

When to go

Lisbon is a full-time fabulous destination. The weather is balmy all year round and there's no shortage of things to do, indoors and out.

SEASONS & CLIMATE

Located at the mouth of the River Tagus, Lisbon's southerly position gives it a Mediterranean feel, though there are around 100 rainy days a year. The river and the Atlantic mean it's not quite as hot here as it is in the Algarve or inland. Although the average temperature from May to September is 20°C (68°F), in July and August this can rise to 30°C (86°F) or more. There is some breeze due to the proximity of the river and the sea but summer is generally a good time to escape to your hotel swimming pool for some cooling off. On the other hand, the average temperature from October to April may only be 10°C (50°F), but it rarely drops below 5°C (41°F). During this time of year, you can expect a mixture of rainy and sunny days when the sky is an impenetrable blue.

ANNUAL EVENTS

There's a lot going on in Lisbon year-round. To help you to find out what takes place and where, here are some annual events and festivals. It's always a good idea to check with the tourist information office (see page 153) when you're planning your visit.

February

Carnival Colourful festivities in the city lead right up to Lent (which begins 25 February in 2009 and 17 February in 2010), and the city develops a particularly Brazilian feel, with carnival floats, fancy dress and dancing.

March

Lisbon Half-Marathon The city shakes off its winter blues with a half-marathon that sees thousands of athletes running through the Parque das Nações (see page 110).
www.lisbon-half-marathon.com

Moda Lisboa Mode-maniacs devour the latest styles from Portugal-based designers at the first of the city's annual fashion shows. www.modalisboa.pt

May–June

Festas de Lisboa/ Festas dos Santos Populares The streets of the Bairro Alto, Chiado, Baixa and Alfama come alive for the popular

Lisbon's Christmas lights reflect in a fountain pool

saints' days, which include special celebrations for St Anthony, St John and St Peter. These areas fill with parades, music and dance, and balconies are decorated with paper lanterns, streamers and coloured lights. Locals give each other gifts of basil pots and paper carnations.

Rock in Rio This popular music festival attracts big-name performers and bands to Lisbon (not Rio) for a five-day fest. www.rockinrio-lisboa.sapo.pt

Sintra Music and Ballet Festival A programme of chamber music and ballet by international performers and some of Portugal's finest talent.

July

Estoril Jazz Festival As the summer starts heating up, this jazz festival attracts plenty of top names.

Cascais Summer Festival A celebration of summer that lights up the area with fireworks and nightly entertainment.

Super Bock Super Rock This metalfest at the Tejo Park regularly attracts some mighty rock names.

August

Jazz em Augusto The Fundação Calouste Gulbenkian (Calouste Gulbenkian Foundation, see page 89) hosts this festival that brings contemporary sounds to the public. www.musica.gulbenkian.pt/jazz

September

Luzboa Biennial (even years) contemporary festival of light that adorns the city's skies and public spaces with different colours and shades. www.luzboa.com

October

Moda Lisboa Fashion hawks can once again check out cutting-edge creations by Portugal-based designers. Ⓦ www.modalisboa.pt

November

Arte Lisboa The capital's contemporary art fair sees artists and galleries from around the world descending on the exhibition centre in the Parque das Nações (see page 110). Ⓦ www.artelisboa.fil.pt

December

Lisbon Marathon This starts every year at the Praça do Comércio (see page 63) and fills the city with spectators. Ⓦ www.lisbon-marathon.com

PUBLIC HOLIDAYS

New Year's Day 1 Jan
Easter 12 Apr 2009; 4 Apr 2010
Liberty Day 25 Apr
Labour Day 1 May
Portugal Day 10 June
Corpus Christi 14 June
Assumption 15 Aug
Republic Day 5 Oct
All Saints' Day 1 Nov
Restoration Day 1 Dec
Day of Our Lady 8 Dec
Christmas Day 25 Dec

Modern architecture

While Lisbon retains plenty of Moorish and Manueline (Portuguese late Gothic) architecture, it's the modern face of its urban furniture that is most captivating. It was after Portugal joined the EU in 1986 that the city really began to change. After the horrific fire in the Chiado in 1988, the area's reconstruction was given over to Portugal's greatest contemporary architect, Álvaro Siza Vieira, who redesigned many of the city's façades and interiors. The highlight of the renovation of the area was the Armazéns do Chiado shopping centre (see page 66).

Another project that changed Lisbon's architectural landscape was the Centro Cultural de Belém (see page 102), a landmark structure designed by architects Manuel Salgado and Vittorio Gregotti. It was controversial when inaugurated in 1992, as the boxy modern building was placed opposite the historical Mosteiro dos Jerónimos (see page 98), blocking its river access.

What really made an indelible imprint on modern-day Lisbon was the reconstruction of the city's neglected eastern waterfront, inspired by the Expo '98 that marked the 500th anniversary of Vasco da Gama's voyage to India. This decaying industrial zone was transformed into the modern and stylish Parque das Nações (see page 110), a social and cultural haven of museums, auditoriums, a conference centre, shops and restaurants, as well as the 17-km (11-mile) Vasco da Gama Bridge. The area's showcase buildings include the award-winning Gare do Oriente (see page 48) by the Spanish star architect Santiago Calatrava.

The state-of-the-art Gare do Oriente

History

Lisbon's turbulent past is full of invasions, occupations and war. When the Romans arrived in the 2nd century AD, they integrated the territory into the empire under the name of Felicitus Jullia, later Olissipo.

The city, which was also known as Lixbuna, Lizhboa and other variations, was taken by the Moors in AD 711. They built houses, mosques and a fortress on the site of what is now the Castelo de São Jorge (see page 74) in Alfama (then called al-Hamma). Arabic became the official language, Islam the official religion, and the city flourished for the next four centuries.

Lisbon was made Portugal's capital in 1260, and a century later the Golden Age of Discovery was beginning. From the 14th to 16th centuries, Portugal's maritime explorers such as Bartolomeu Dias and Vasco da Gama forged routes to sail around the Cape of Good Hope and to the Americas.

Gold was discovered in Brazil, and, while the Portuguese royal family grew rich from its colonial pickings, life on the city's streets wasn't so glorious. In 1506, around 2,000 Jews were massacred on the streets. Growing colonial unrest led to the Wars of Restoration, during which a group of noblemen laid siege to Lisbon in 1640. The Duke of Bragança was crowned King Dom João IV, but Spain would not recognise Portuguese independence until 1668.

It wasn't until 1755, when the Great Earthquake (and tsunami that followed) devastated the city killing 90,000 people, that ideals began to change. After what became known as the first modern disaster, the Marquês de Pombal rebuilt Lisbon by bringing the city centre into the Age of Enlightenment, though poor areas such as the Alfama remained medieval.

After suffering Napoleonic invasions and civil war during the 19th century, Portugal experienced a major turn of events when its king Dom Carlos I was assassinated in 1908. His successor, Dom Manuel II, lasted only until the Republican revolution of October 1910. The country remained unsettled until the 1926 coup d'état and the subsequent rise of Dr António de Oliveira Salazar to prime minister in 1932, who then led a 48-year dictatorship during which he imposed a somewhat repressive regime which he called the Estado Novo (New State). Establishing the true nature of Salazar's dictatorship – and the extent to which it was good or bad for Portugal – is a vexed and shifting question. Although he voiced admiration for some far-right leaders of other countries, he prevented his own from drifting too far in that direction. The Estado Novo effectively ended in 1968, when serious illness finally caused Salazar to step down.

The 1960s had already seen unrest in the colonies, gradual liberalisation of the press, and socialist cultural movements. The highlight of Portugal's transition to democracy was a bloodless coup known as the Carnation Revolution. At 12.25 on 25 April 1974, the banned protest song *Grândola, Vila Morena* was broadcast on the radio and soldiers entered the streets of Lisbon with red carnations protruding from their tanks.

Since then Portugal has pulled itself out of the past and its capital has been transformed once again. Portugal joined the EU in 1986, and Lisbon was the European Capital of Culture in 1994. The city hosted Expo '98 and, in 2004, the European Football Championships. Although the economy still struggles, these events have led to massive investment and renewed confidence, and, as the first decade of the 21st century draws to a close, Lisbon is now a firmly established, magnificently attractive, city-break destination.

Lifestyle

A famous saying in Portugal is that 'Lisbon plays, Porto works and Braga prays'. While people in Lisbon also work and pray, it is a vibrant metropolis with a laid-back café culture and lively nightlife.

This is a capital city with a busy financial district where socialising is important. Rather than belonging to international café chains, the numerous coffee shops of Lisbon are individual. There are cafés where people spend an hour chatting to friends and sipping *um galão* (milky coffee in a glass) and others where they stand at the counter for a quick snack such as *pastel de nata* (Portuguese custard tart). There are also internet cafés and coffee kiosks in the street.

Although there are sandwich bars in Lisbon, people can take two hours for lunch in order to eat properly, so you'll often find that the shops and some museums close at this time. Portions tend to be large, but don't be afraid of leaving a little on your plate – they'll take it as a compliment that they've fed you enough! In some places you can order a main course to share between two people.

Generally the Portuguese are very polite, so unless you're very familiar, you should say *bom día* (good morning) or *boa tarde* (good afternoon) rather than *olá*. You're unlikely to see anyone taking their shoes off in a public place, except on the beach, as it's considered bad manners.

The Portuguese do like a drink and, in fact, have a very high national average of alcohol consumption. However, you're unlikely to see drunken Portuguese falling out of the bars as in some other countries. Even though locals tend to go out late at night, even the younger people can spend hours pondering over one drink before heading on to a club after midnight. It's all about taking your time and enjoying the food, wine, good company and surroundings more than the actual alcohol content. There's no rush – just enjoy yourself!

Stop and unwind at a café in leafy Parque Eduardo VII

Culture

Fado remains at the forefront of Lisbon's musical identity. Whether you love or hate the melancholic sounds of *fado* music, it attracts thousands of tourists and locals to the restaurants and bars of the Bairro Alto and Alfama every year.

There are two forms of *fado*: one form developed among the privileged students of the University of Coimbra, while the other arose among the working classes in Lisbon and was sung by social outcasts. It was often called *fado do marinhero* (sailors' song), referring to the seafarers during the Golden Age of Discovery who yearned for their homeland.

Fado is sung by a solo vocalist and usually accompanied by a *viola* (Spanish guitar) and a *guitarra* (pear-shaped, 12-string Portuguese guitar). Lisbon's most famous *fadista* is Amália Rodrigues (see page 101), who rose to fame in the 1950s and 1960s, but others have followed in her wake.

Aside from *fado*, Lisbon is home to the Orquestra and Coro Gulbenkian (see page 20), has a thriving jazz scene, popular music venues and several music festivals (see page 10). There is plenty of dance in the city, too, from performances by the Companhia Nacional do Bailado to shows by contemporary dance groups.

The Baixa, Chiado and Bairro Alto were once the favourite haunts of artists and writers, and today you'll find monuments to Luís de Camões and Fernando Pessoa in these areas. Outside A Brasileira café (see page 67) in the Bairro Alto is a seated statue of Pessoa; he used to frequent the café which is still popular with arty types who meet there for a daily chat.

Mother and child statue in Parque Eduardo VII

When it comes to the visual arts, Lisbon boasts the Fundação Calouste Gulbenkian (Calouste Gulbenkian Foundation, see page 89), the premier arts organisation in Portugal and home to the Orquestra Gulbenkian and Coro Gulbenkian, as well as the Museu Calouste Gulbenkian and Centro de Arte Moderna José de Azeredo Perdigão (see page 90). Beside that, Centro Cultural de Belém (see page 102), the largest and one of the most popular contemporary arts venues in the city, houses the Museu do Design and hosts regular exhibitions by international artists in its galleries, as well as putting on opera, ballet, classical music and jazz concerts in its Performance Centre. The Museu Nacional de Arte Antiga (see page 103) is considered one of the most important museums in the country. Located in a 17th-century palace, it showcases a stellar collection of 15th- to 19th-century Portuguese and European paintings. Museu do Chiado (see page 64) was Lisbon's first modern art gallery and has an impressive collection of works by Portugal's most representative 20th- and 21st-century artists.

For the performing arts, Teatro Camões (see page 114) in the Parque das Nações is one of the city's newest theatres, and is home to the Companhia Nacional do Bailado, the country's national ballet company. Teatro Nacional Dona Maria II (see page 64), historically one of the city's most important theatres, presents a programme of theatre, circus and performance art. Teatro Nacional de São Carlos (see page 65), with its stunning rococo interior, replaced the pre-1755 building that previously stood there. It has an extensive repertoire of opera, classical music and theatre.

A world map mosaic in Belém

MAKING THE MOST OF Lisbon

Shopping

Lisbon has an alluring profusion of boutiques, markets, regular street shops and large shopping centres. In the Baixa-Chiado area, particularly along the Rua Augusta, there's a mix of international chain stores, as well as small traditional shops selling leather goods, jewellery and handicrafts. For funky boutiques and offbeat fashions, check out the storefronts of Bairro Alto. Indulge your penchant for designer labels on the Avenida da Liberdade or opt for the traditional shopping area on the Campo de Ourique (see page 92). There's a branch of the Spanish department store El Corte Inglés in Alto del Parque Eduardo VII. The downtown shopping centre of Armazéns do Chiado (see page 66), with a FNAC and a series of food outlets, is a favoured retail destination. **Amoreiras** (www.amoreiras.com) and **Colombo** (www.colombo.pt) are both popular shopping centres, but the newest is Centro Comercial Vasco da Gama (see page 114) in Parque das Nações, with 164 shops on four floors.

When it comes to what to buy, there's a good choice of leather goods, lace and linen. Look out for copper dishes, painted terracotta ceramics and *azulejos* tiles. From the supermarket you can pick up a selection of *presunto* (smoked ham), *chouriço* (spicy sausage), wines from Estremadura, Beiras, Dão and the Douro, port wine from the Douro and *vinho verde* (young white wine) from the Minho.

Souvenirs rule the roost here ...

There are small, sometimes impromptu, markets dotted all around the city. The Feira da Ladra is a flea market in the Alfama, and if you like to rummage among gems and junk, it is open for action every Tuesday and Saturday. There's also a fish market in Cais do Sodré, selling everything from the wet pulp of octopus to *bacalhau* (salt codfish).

If you intend to do some serious shopping while you're in town you should consider investing in a Lisboa Shopping Card. This lasts for either 24 (€3.70) or 72 hours (€5.80) and can be purchased from the tourist office (Lisbon Welcome Centre, see page 153). It gives up to 15 per cent off in more than 200 shops in the Baixa, Chiado and Avenida da Liberdade.

USEFUL SHOPPING PHRASES

What time do the shops open/close?
A que horas abrem/fecham as lojas?
A kee orah abrayng/fayshown ash lohzhash?

How much is this?
Quanto custa isto?
Kwantoo kooshta eeshtoo?

Can I try this on?
Posso provar este?
Possoo proovahr aysht?

My size is ...
O meu tamanho (número) é ...
Oo mayo tamanyo (noomiroo) eh ...

I'll take this one, thank you
Levo este, obrigado
Lehvoo aysht, ohbreegahdoo

This is too large/too small/too expensive. Do you have any others?
Este é muito grande/muito pequeno/muito caro. Tem outros?
Aysht eh muingtoo grangdi/muingtoo pikaynoo/muingtoo kahroo. Tayng ohtroosh?

Eating & drinking

Eating in Lisbon is a real pleasure, as the Portuguese love their food, menus are full of variety and portions are generous.

Traditional Portuguese restaurants compete with a large number of international eateries. Try one of the Brazilian restaurants, which often have buffet menus that include cold meats and fish, as well as hot meat from the spit. There are plenty of pizzerias, steak houses, Chinese and even a few Indian restaurants, as well as the usual choice of fast food and sandwiches. Vegetarians sometimes find it easier to eat in the international restaurants, as the local diet doesn't regularly include options for non-meat eaters; a smattering of vegetarian restaurants does exist, though.

Lisbon's proximity to the sea means that fish and seafood feature high on the menu, but there are plenty of meat dishes as well. Soup is the mainstay of the Portuguese diet and you'll find it on many menus as a starter, particularly *caldo verde* (a delicious cabbage soup made from chicken stock and a slice of the spicy *chouriço* sausage) and *sopa de legumes* (vegetable soup).

Bacalhau (salt cod) is a common local speciality and you'll often see it hanging up in the shops. The most popular salt codfish recipe is *bacalhau com natas*, salt codfish with cream and potatoes. Squid (*lulas*) is another staple and often fried in batter – the larger ones in rings and

PRICE CATEGORIES

Restaurant ratings in this book are based on the average price of a two-course dinner for one without drinks:

£ up to €20 **££** €20–35 **£££** over €35

RESTAURANT CARD

The Lisboa Restaurant Card is valid for 72 hours and can be purchased from the tourist office (Lisbon Welcome Centre, see page 153). It offers discounts of up to ten per cent in around 45 quality Lisbon restaurants.

the baby squid fried whole, which are delicious as the legs go all crispy. Also look out for *camarão* (prawns), *gambas grelhadas* (grilled king prawns), *caldeirada* (fish stew), *lulas recheadas* (stuffed squid), *polvo grelhado* (grilled octopus), *sardinhas assadas* (grilled sardines), *robalo* (sea bass) and *sargo* (sea bream). These will often be served with *batatas* (potatoes), *batatas fritas* (chips), *salada mixta* (mixed salad) with *azeitonas* (olives) or vegetables such as *espinafres* (spinach).

Meat also features high on the menu and includes *bife tornedo* (succulent, quite rare piece of beef), *bifes de Perú* (turkey steak), *cabrito assado* (grilled kid), *costeleta de vitela* (veal cutlets/chops),

Traditional bacalhau *is widely available and delicious*

frango no churrasco (barbecued chicken), *leitão assado* (spit-roast suckling pig) and *lombo de porco assado* (roast pork).

Many of the desserts and cakes are made with eggs, including *pasteis de nata* or *pasteis de Belém* (custard tart), *papos de anjo* (egg-based pastry dish) and *pudim* (crème caramel).

Cafés are your best option for less formal dining; try one of the *cervejarias* (café/bar) for snacks such as *tosta mixta* (toasted cheese and ham sandwiches) or surf 'n' turf of steak with crab claws (they'll give you a hammer to crack them). Some restaurants will automatically put a basket of bread and cheeses or fish pastes in front of you, but unless you want to eat and pay for these, you should ask them to take them away.

There are many ways to drink coffee: *uma bica* (small coffee, like an espresso), *um meia de leite* (coffee with milk), *um garoto* (small coffee with milk) and *um galão* (milky coffee in a tall glass). You can also order *chá* (tea) but you'll have to ask for *leite* (milk). There are plenty of regional wines in Portugal, including from the Estremadura region

You're never far from a good coffee shop in Chiado

(around Lisbon), Beiras, Dão, Douro (where port wine comes from) and the Minho (where the young, slightly tangy *vinho verde* is produced).

USEFUL DINING PHRASES

I would like a table for ... people
Queria uma mesa para ... pessoas
Kireea ooma mehza para ... pesoash

May I have the bill, please?
Pode-me dar a conta, por favor?
Pohd-mi dahr er kohngta, poor favohr?

Waiter/waitress!
Faz favor!
Fash favohr!

Could I have it well-cooked/medium/rare, please?
Posso escolher bem passado/médio/mal passado, por favor?
Possoo ishkoolyer bayng pasahdoo/medio/mahl pasahdoo, poor favohr?

I am a vegetarian. Does this contain meat?
Sou vegetariano/a. Isto tem carne?
Soh vezhetahreeahnoo/a. Ishtoo tehng kahrni?

Where is the toilet (restroom) please?
Por favor, onde são os lavabos?
Poor favohr, ohngdee sowng oos lavahboosh?

I would like a cup of/two cups of/another coffee/tea
Queria uma chávena de/duas chávenas de/outro café/chá
Kireea ooma shahvna di/dooash shahvnash di/ohtroo kafeh/shah

Entertainment & nightlife

There's no shortage of entertainment in Lisbon, but don't expect the Portuguese to be falling out of the pubs. They know how to have fun, but generally stay well in control. Part of the reason is that they eat well and drink slowly. Dinner can be taken around 20.00 or 21.00 and accompanied by music in a *fado* bar, or you can enjoy a drink before heading out to a club.

Clubs don't generally get going until midnight. You can wine, dine and dance all over the city but the labyrinthine streets of Bairro Alto, such as Rua Diário de Noticias and the adjacent alleys, are traditionally the most popular place to go out drinking and clubbing. The Alfama is less of a party area, with the exception of the city's most famous club, the Lux Bar (see page 83) by Santa Apolónia Station.

Two areas have transformed nightlife in Lisbon: the Parque das Nações (see page 110) and Alcântara. The first has a long line of riverfront restaurant-bars, some of which become clubs later in the evening. Alcântara and the former Docas (docks) by 25 de Abril Bridge include some of the city's trendiest restaurants, bars and nightclubs.

There are multiplex cinemas in the large shopping centres such as Amoreiras (see page 22) and Colombo (see page 22). Most films are shown in their original language with subtitles. **Londres** cinema (ⓐ Avenida de Roma 7A ⓣ (21) 840 1313) and Cinemateca Portuguesa (see page 84) show arthouse films.

Lisbon offers a good choice of live music, including *fado* clubs where you can eat and drink, jazz clubs such as the Hot Clube de Portugal (see page 95), Speakeasy and Blues Café (see page 108), as well as larger venues, such as the Coliseu dos Recreios (see page 89) and Pavilhão Atlântico (see page 113), where international bands play. Coliseu dos Recreios is a frequent venue for both popular music

Balmy evenings in the Bairro Alto

and classical concerts. There are also open-air events throughout the year. The tourist office publishes *Follow Me*, a monthly magazine in English that highlights forthcoming live events and festivals.

Tickets for live events can be bought from FNAC bookshops (in most shopping centres), or on-line at www.fnac.pt or www.ticketline.pt

Evening dining and entertainment at the Casino Estoril *(see page 122)*

Fado houses with live entertainment daily are dotted around the Bairro Alto (see page 69) and the Alfama (see page 81), and retain their popularity both with locals and tourists.

Theatre might not be the best live entertainment unless your Portuguese is particularly good. However, most of the large theatres in Lisbon also have a decent programme of classical concerts, opera and ballet (see Culture, pages 18–20).

Sport & relaxation

SPECTATOR SPORTS

Football The Portuguese love football, whether it's played by an international outfit, a Superliga team or a local club. There are two Superliga teams in Lisbon: **Sport Lisboa e Benfica** (ⓦ www.slbenfica.pt) and **Sporting Clube de Portugal** (ⓦ www.sporting.pt). Benfica is based at the Estádio da Luz (see page 84), while Sporting Clube de Portugal is based at the **Estádio José de Alvalade** (ⓐ Rua Professor Fernando da Fonseca ⓣ (21) 751 6000). While it can be difficult to get tickets for the larger matches, you might be able to buy a ticket on the day of the match from the stadium (see ⓦ www.fpf.pt).

Racing The **Estoril Race Track** (ⓐ Av. Alfredo Cesar Torres Alcabideche, Estoril ⓦ www.circuito-estoril.pt) is a Formula One circuit and hosts car and motorbike racing throughout most of the year.

PARTICIPATION SPORTS

Horse riding There are several places to go horse riding, including the **Quinta da Marinha** resort (ⓣ (21) 486 0100 ⓦ www.quintadamarinha.pt/centrohipico), the **Manuel Possolo** school in the Parque Municipal de Gandarinha (ⓣ (21) 482 1720) and the **Centro Hípico da Costa do Estoril** (ⓣ (21) 487 2064 ⓦ www.centrohipicocostaestoril.com).

Sailing & watersports There are sailing and watersports schools dotted all along the beach from Cascais Marina to Oeiras, as well as the Sintra coast further north. The most popular sport among the younger crowd is surfing, and for this Carcavelos is one of the best places, along with Guincho and Colares. You can hire equipment and have lessons with **SuperWind** in Oeiras (ⓣ (21) 469 4602), **Surfing**

Clube de Portugal in São Pedro de Estoril (ⓣ (21) 466 4516) and **Windsurf Café** in Carcavelos (ⓣ (21) 457 8965), or catch a few waves on your own board. Most of these schools offer windsurfing and body boarding as well.

Tennis Tennis can be played at the **Quinta da Marinha** resort (ⓣ (21) 486 0180) and the **Clube de Ténis de Estoril** (ⓣ (21) 466 2770) on Avenida Conde de Barcelona, which has 18 floodlit courts and often hosts international matches.

RELAXATION

Golf Estoril has quite a concentration of top-notch golf courses, including the **Estoril Golf Course** (ⓣ (21) 468 0054), **Penha Longa** (ⓣ (21) 924 9031 ⓦ www.penhalonga.com), **Quinta da Marinha** (ⓣ (21) 486 0180 ⓦ www.quintadamarinha.pt) and **Oitavos Golf** (ⓣ (21) 486 0600 ⓦ www.quintadamarinha-oitavosgolfe.pt).

Lisbon's Estádio José de Alvalade is known for its multicoloured seats

Accommodation

Lisbon has a diverse range of accommodation, from luxury 5-star hotels with pools to mid-range 3-star hotels and *residenciais* (bed and breakfast).

There is plenty of accommodation available around the Bairro Alto and Chiado, including some of the city's trendiest (and most expensive) hotels, alongside budget options. This area is ideal if you're after a party weekend, as it won't be far to get back to your hotel from either the Bairro Alto or the Docas.

The hotels in the streets around Parque Eduardo VII and Amoreiras are favoured for business trips, but don't let this put you off if you want to be in a quieter part of town.

Parque das Nações (see page 110) is also popular for business with its easy access to the airport and the Feira Internacional de Lisboa (FIL), the city's conference centre. It is also good for children, as it features several attractions for kids, plus you are close to shopping, eating and drinking venues. However, if you are looking for some surf, you might prefer to stay out of Lisbon in Cascais or Estoril (see page 130), which have easier access to the beach. Here you'll find everything from camping and small hotels to resort and apartment hotels.

For romantic weekends, there are manor houses, historic and boutique hotels in Sintra, Chiado and Alfama. Portugal's *pousadas*,

PRICE CATEGORIES

The price symbols indicate the approximate price of a double room for two people, including breakfast:

£ up to €100 **££** €100–235 **£££** over €235

luxury hotels housed in converted historic buildings such as churches, palaces, monasteries and fortresses, are also popular. The nearest ones to Lisbon are in Queluz, towards Sintra (see page 142), and just outside Setúbal, so this is a better option if you are staying longer and want to go exploring. For ideas see Ⓦ www.pousadas.pt. Also look out for *estalagems*, state-run hotels.

You can easily book hotels on-line at a number of websites, many of which offer reasonable discounts. As well as Ⓦ www.expedia.com and Ⓦ www.hotels.com, try Ⓦ www.maisturismo.com for a range of accommodation, Ⓦ www.heritage.pt for historic boutique hotels in Lisbon, Ⓦ www.solaresdeportugal.pt for manor houses and Ⓦ www.portugalvirtual.pt for *residenciais*. It can sometimes be cheaper to book directly. If you find yourself without accommodation, contact the tourist office or head to the Bairro Alto or Chiado area and try one of the *residenciais*.

HOTELS & GUEST HOUSES

Hotel Anjo Azul £ Cosy four-floor hotel at the heart of Bairro Alto, with 20 simple but well-equipped rooms on a scenic street. Ⓐ Rua Luz Soriano 75 Ⓣ (21) 347 8069 Ⓦ www.anjoazul.com Ⓣ Metro: Baixa-Chiado; Tram: 28

Hotel Nacional £ A comfortable hotel within easy reach of the Praça do Marquês de Pombal, with private bathrooms, buffet breakfast room and a bar. Ⓐ Rua Castilho 34 Ⓣ (21) 355 4433 Ⓦ www.hotel-nacional.com Ⓣ Metro: Marquês de Pombai; Bus: 22, 48

Residencial Dom Sancho I £ Conveniently located for the Bairro Alto and Alfama, this is a family-run hotel. Rooms have private bathrooms, there's a breakfast room decorated with *azulejos*, and room service.

ⓐ Av. da Liberdade 202 ⓣ (21) 354 8648 ⓦ www.domsancho.com
ⓝ Metro: Restauradores; Bus: 2, 9, 36, 44, 711, 732

Residencial Florescente £ This friendly hotel is located just off Praça dos Restauradores, close to the Baixa and Bairro Alto, as well as the metro station. There are various-sized rooms, all with en suite bathrooms. ⓐ Rua das Portas de Santo Antão 99, 3rd and 4th floors ⓣ (21) 342 6609 ⓦ www.residencialflorescente.com ⓝ Metro: Restauradores

Hotel Açores Lisboa ££ A contemporary hotel in the financial district, five minutes from the Praça do Marquês de Pombal and right by the metro station at Praça de Espanha. Facilities include a restaurant, bar, terrace, TV lounge, business centre and private indoor car park. ⓐ Av. Columbano Bordalo Pinheiro 3 ⓣ (21) 722 2920 ⓦ www.bensaude.pt ⓝ Metro: Praça de Espanha

Hotel Dom Pedro Lisboa ££ Located opposite the Amoreiras shopping centre, this tall hotel in mirrored blue glass is close to the business centre. A modern deluxe hotel, it showcases stunning views across the city. ⓐ Av. Engenheiro Duarte Pacheco 24 ⓣ (21) 389 6600 ⓦ www.dompedro.com ⓝ Metro: Rato; Bus: 83, 718

Hotel Miraparque ££ This hotel overlooks the Parque Eduardo VII and has a quiet location. It also has its own restaurant and bar. ⓐ Av. Sidónio Pais 12 ⓣ (21) 352 4286 ⓦ www.miraparque.com ⓝ Metro: Marquês de Pombal; Bus: 22, 48

Hotel Tivoli Oriente ££ A modern hotel in the Parque das Nações, opposite the Centro Comercial Vasco da Gama and ten minutes from the airport. There's a heated indoor pool, health club, bar and two

A modern suite in the Hotel Açores Lisboa

restaurants. ⓐ Av. Dom João II ⓣ (21) 891 5100 ⓦ www.tivolihotels.com ⓝ Metro: Oriente

As Janelas Verdes £££ Once the home of Portuguese writer Eça de Queiroz, this former 18th-century mansion still has a library on the top floor. It has pretty gardens and is located near the river by the Museu Nacional de Arte Antiga. ⓐ Rua das Janelas Verdes 47 ⓣ (21) 396 8143 ⓦ www.asjanelasverdes.com ⓝ Tram: 15; Bus: 28, 706, 714, 727

Bairro Alto Hotel £££ A stylish boutique hotel in the heart of the old city, it has easy access to cultural attractions as well as shopping and nightlife. All of its 55 rooms are kitted out in the latest technology and swank design; there's also a rooftop bar, restaurant, lobby

lounge and fitness room. Praça Luís de Camões 2 (21) 340 8222 www.bairroaltohotel.com Metro: Baixa-Chiado

Hotel Avenida Palace £££ The first palace hotel in the city, it is located by Praça dos Restauradores and is convenient to the Baixa, Bairro Alto and Avenida da Liberdade. Rua 1 de Dezembro 123 (21) 321 8100 www.hotelavenidapalace.pt Metro: Rossio

The sumptuous foyer in the Hotel Avenida Palace

Hotel Britânia £££ Designed by famous Portuguese modernist architect Cassiano Branco in the 1940s, this renovated boutique hotel features art deco décor. Ideally located on a quiet street just off the Avenida da Liberdade. ⓐ Rua Rodrigues Sampaio 17 ⓣ (21) 315 5016 ⓦ www.hotel-britania.com ⓝ Metro: Restauradores

Hotel Jerónimos 8 £££ This design hotel at the heart of historic Belém features ultra-stylish rooms with modern amenities and a swanky bar. ⓐ Rua dos Jerónimos 8 ⓣ (21) 360 0900 ⓦ www.jeronimos8.com ⓝ Tram: 15; Bus: 714, 727, 751

Lapa Palace £££ A former aristocrat's palace built in 1870, this luxury hotel is set on a hill amid tropical gardens with spectacular views of the river and city. There are outdoor and indoor heated pools and a spa. ⓐ Rua do Pau de Bandeira 4 ⓣ (21) 394 9494 ⓦ www.lapa-palace.com ⓝ Tram: 25; Bus: 713

Palácio Belmonte £££ A 14th-century palace, this romantic hotel is located in the Alfama by the Castelo de São Jorge. The refurbishment has maintained the ancient beams and 18th-century tiles. Each suite has been individually designed and named after a Portuguese personality. ⓐ Páteo Dom Fradique 14 ⓣ (21) 881 6600 ⓦ www.palaciobelmonte.com ⓝ Tram: 28, 18, 12; Bus: 37

Solar do Castelo £££ This delightful hotel in a historic mansion is located within the walls of the Castelo de São Jorge. Known as the Kitchen Mansion, it was constructed where the kitchens of the former Alcaçova Palace once stood. ⓐ Rua das Cozinhas 2 ⓣ (21) 880 6050 ⓦ www.solardocastelo.com ⓝ Tram: 28, 18, 12; Bus: 37

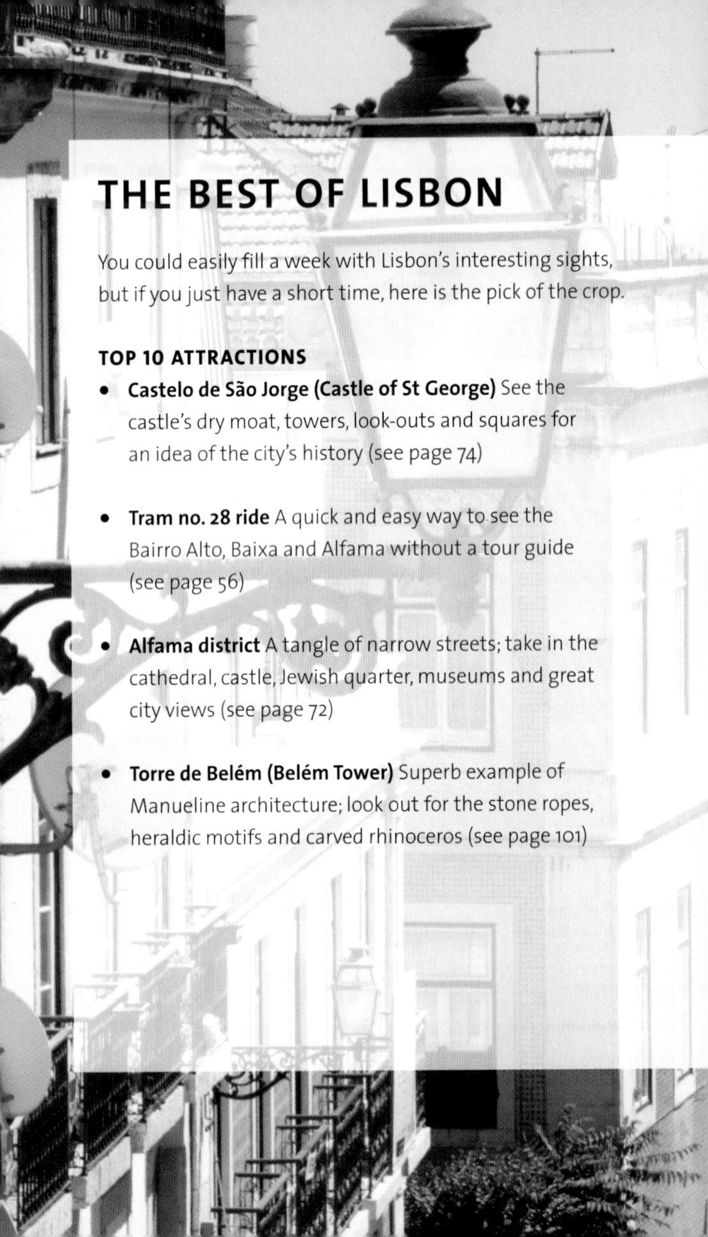

THE BEST OF LISBON

You could easily fill a week with Lisbon's interesting sights, but if you just have a short time, here is the pick of the crop.

TOP 10 ATTRACTIONS

- **Castelo de São Jorge (Castle of St George)** See the castle's dry moat, towers, look-outs and squares for an idea of the city's history (see page 74)
- **Tram no. 28 ride** A quick and easy way to see the Bairro Alto, Baixa and Alfama without a tour guide (see page 56)
- **Alfama district** A tangle of narrow streets; take in the cathedral, castle, Jewish quarter, museums and great city views (see page 72)
- **Torre de Belém (Belém Tower)** Superb example of Manueline architecture; look out for the stone ropes, heraldic motifs and carved rhinoceros (see page 101)

- **Mosteiro dos Jerónimos (Hieronymites Monastery)** Architectural masterpiece in historic Belém (see page 98)
- **Fundação Calouste Gulbenkian (Calouste Gulbenkian Foundation)** Modern art, lush gardens and musical history in the making (see page 89)
- **Elevador de Santa Justa** Ride the elevator for great views over the Baixa (see page 60)
- **Museu Nacional de Arte Antiga (National Museum of Ancient Art)** A green-shuttered 17th-century palace of art (see page 103)
- **Baixa district** Thrash that credit card into submission in this shopaholics' paradise (see page 58)
- **Museu Nacional do Azulejo (National Tile Museum)** A 16th-century former convent with a superb collection of *azulejos* (see page 80)

Alfama is bursting with exciting vistas

Suggested itineraries

HALF-DAY: LISBON IN A HURRY

Jump on the vintage tram no. 28 (see page 56), which clatters along the narrow streets through several key districts. There are *paragems* (stops) along the route in Campo Ourique, Estrela, Bairro Alto, Baixa, Alfama and Martim Moniz. Hop off at Alfama and visit Castelo de São Jorge (see page 74) to take in its spectacular city views. If you have time, stop for a coffee in the Largo das Portas do Sol before heading back.

1 DAY: TIME TO SEE A LITTLE MORE

Again, take tram no. 28 up to the Alfama and visit the Castelo de São Jorge, but stop for lunch in or around the castle. Wind your way back downhill past the Jewish quarter and the **Casa dos Bicos** (ⓐ Rua dos Bacalhoeiros), then head along to the Baixa for a spot of shopping. If your feet are tired from Lisbon's hills, take the Elevador de Glória (see page 60) from Praça dos Restauradores up to the Bairro Alto and walk round to the Solar do Vinho do Porto (see page 71) where you can sink into an armchair with a well-earned glass of port.

2–3 DAYS: TIME TO SEE MUCH MORE

A little bit of extra time means that you can really explore the one-day options suggested above, and maybe linger in particular districts. Spend some time soaking up the atmosphere of the Bairro Alto and Chiado, visiting the Convento do Carmo (see page 58) and Museu do Chiado (see page 64) and making time for its cafés and for a very Portuguese evening of *fado*, before heading off to a club in the renovated Docas. A whole day is needed to take in the sights of Belém. The Mosteiro dos Jerónimos (see page 98) and Torre de Belém (see page 101) should be at the very top of your list, but make sure you don't miss

the Centro Cultural de Belém (see page 102), and the Padrão dos Descobrimentos (Discoveries Monument, see page 99). Another day could easily be spent in the Parque das Nações (see page 110) with its superb Oceanário de Lisboa (Lisbon Oceanarium, see page 110), Teleférico (cable car, see page 112) and the huge Centro Comercial Vasco da Gama (see page 114), as well as plenty of riverside restaurants and bars.

LONGER: ENJOYING LISBON TO THE FULL

Visit the Fundação Calouste Gulbenkian (see page 89), find a retreat in one of the city parks, such as the lush Jardim Botânico (see page 86) and Parque Eduardo VII (see page 87), or take a boat trip on the River Tagus. Make time for a trip to Sintra (see page 132) to see the Castelo dos Mouros and the Palácio da Pena, or head to Cascais and Estoril (see page 120) for beaches, watersports, golf, a young crowd and plenty of vibrant nightlife.

The gorgeously manicured gardens at the Fronteira Palace (see page 86)

Something for nothing

Exploring Lisbon on foot is a tiring but worthwhile experience. As it is built on seven hills – Castelo, Estrela, Graça, Monte, Penha de França, Santa Catarina (see page 63) and São Pedro de Alcântara – it gives you a vista of the city at no cost. At various points around the city, *miradouros* (belvederes or viewing points) have been built to enhance the view and let you relax as you take in the sights.

After climbing the steep Alfama streets to the Castelo de São Jorge (see page 74), you'll be rewarded with fabulous views from the first castle square across the Baixa and Chiado. Look out for the ruins of the Convento do Carmo (see page 58), the domes of Igreja de Santa Engrácia (see page 74) and **Basilica de Estrela** (ⓐ Largo da Estrela) as well as the Parque Eduardo VII (see page 87) and the River Tagus. Just a walk downhill from the castle, you'll find two adjacent viewing points, Portas da Sol and Santa Luzia (see page 77), from where you can peer over the rooftops of the Alfama to the river. At Santa Luzia, look for the old *azulejos* tiles to see an image of Lisbon prior to the 1755 earthquake.

On the other side of the hill, on Largo da Graça, is another viewing point (see page 77) with similar views as the castle. It's much more romantic here and you can look up towards the castle, relax in the shade of the pine trees and gaze over the rooftops of the Mouraria quarter.

Walk to the top of the slanting Parque Eduardo VII to have a well-defined view of the park's formal gardens and straight down the Avenida da Liberdade.

From the *miradouro* at São Pedro de Alcântara (see page 63) in the Bairro Alto, there's a panoramic view of the castle, Baixa and Avenida da Liberdade. For a view in the opposite direction, head to

Santa Catarina (see page 63) at the other end of the Bairro Alto, from where you can see the Basilica da Estrela, the districts of Lapa and Madragoa and over the roofs to the port.

There are priceless views from the city's miradouros

When it rains

There are so many museums, cultural and historic sites and other attractions in Lisbon that you won't be short of things to do if it rains. Although the weather is generally fair, it does rain from time to time and you don't want to be caught slipping down the cobbled streets through Alfama (see page 72) or heading for the beach in Cascais (see page 126). With the help of the efficient metro system and trams, you can zip across the city from one attraction to the next.

The Museu Calouste Gulbenkian (see page 90) and the Centro de Arte Moderna (see page 90) are a good place to start. You could easily spend a day looking round them both – and there's a restaurant to stop for lunch. Then if it stops raining you can head straight outdoors to the lush Gulbenkian gardens or walk back to town through the Parque Eduardo VII (see page 87).

If you're caught in a shower in the Bairro Alto, head downhill to see the Museu do Chiado's modern art collection (see page 64) or immerse yourself in a long lunch at one of the area's numerous restaurants.

You could spend a few hours in the Museu Nacional de Arte Antiga (see page 103), where the collection of Portuguese painting will keep you intrigued. Also the Docas are not far away if you want to spend some time under cover eating and drinking until the rain stops.

Another option is Belém (see page 96). You can hop from the Mosteiro dos Jerónimos (see page 98) next door to the Museu Nacional de Arqueologia (see page 103) and the Museu de Marinha (see page 102), or nip over the road to the Centro Cultural de Belém (see page 102), with its contemporary exhibitions, Museu de Design and restaurant.

Alternatively, spend the day indulging yourself in one of the shopping centres, which generally open from 10.00 until midnight – there are metro stations at Colombo and Centro Comercial Vasco da Gama (see page 114). You can stay for lunch here too, and this doesn't necessarily mean settling for fast food – there are quality restaurants alongside sandwich and coffee bars.

If you opt for the Parque das Nações (see page 110), you could see the wonders of the underwater world at the Oceanário de Lisboa (see page 110) and discover something scientific at the Pavilhão do Conhecimento (see page 112), a particularly good option if you're with children.

The Centro Comercial Vasco da Gama is a great place to spend a rainy day

On arrival

TIME DIFFERENCE

Portugal follows Greenwich Mean Time (GMT). During Daylight Saving Time (late Mar–late Sept), the clocks are put forward by one hour.

ARRIVING

By air

Aeroporto de Portela (t (21) 841 3500 w www.ana.pt), Lisbon's international airport, is located in the north of the city and is the busiest and most important airport in the country. You will find a tourist information booth in the arrivals terminal. If you want to take a taxi into the city centre, you should buy a voucher here. However, the quick and efficient AEROBUS runs every 20 minutes from the airport to Cais do Sodré via Saldanha, Marquês Pombal, Avenida da Liberdade, Restauradores, Rossio and Praça do Comércio. Tickets can be purchased onboard and cost €1.35 for a single with the Lisboa Card (see page 53) or €3.35 otherwise. There are also a few local buses, including no. 5 direct to Parque das Nações (see page 110), and an hourly Airport Shuttle Bus to Cascais/Estoril (€8.50).

By rail

Portugal's Alfa-Pendular trains are the best ones to take if travelling long distances. Clean, fast and reasonably priced, these run to Faro in the south and Coimbra, Porto and Braga in the north, with a few stops in between. Long-distance trains leave from **Gare do Oriente** (a Av. Dom João II) and **Santa Apolónia** (a Av. Infante Dom Henrique) stations, while trains to Cascais/Estoril leave from **Cais do Sodré**

(ⓐ Cais do Sodré) and to Sintra from **Entrecampos** (ⓐ Rua Dr Eduardo Neves). The phone number for all railway stations is ⓣ (21) 318 5900. For more information, see the Portuguese railway site ⓦ www.cp.pt

By road

There are two main coach terminals in Lisbon, one in Gare do Oriente in Parque das Nações (see opposite) and the other in **Sete Rios** (ⓐ Estrada de Benfica). For more information on coach transport, see Rede Expressos ⓦ www.rede-expressos.pt

IF YOU GET LOST, TRY ...

Excuse me, do you speak English?
Desculpe, fala Inglês?
Dishkoolper, fahla eenglaysh?

Excuse me, is this the right way to ... the cathedral/the tourist office/the castle/the old town?
Desculpe, é este o caminho certo para ... a catedral/o departamento de turismo/o castelo/a cidade velha?
Dishkoolper, eh aysht oo kameenyo sehrtoo para ... er katidrahl/ oo dehpartamehntoo deh tooreesmoo/oo kastehloo/ er seedahd vehlya?

Can you point to it on my map?
Pode indicá-lo no meu mapa?
Pohd eendeecahloo noo mayo mahpa?

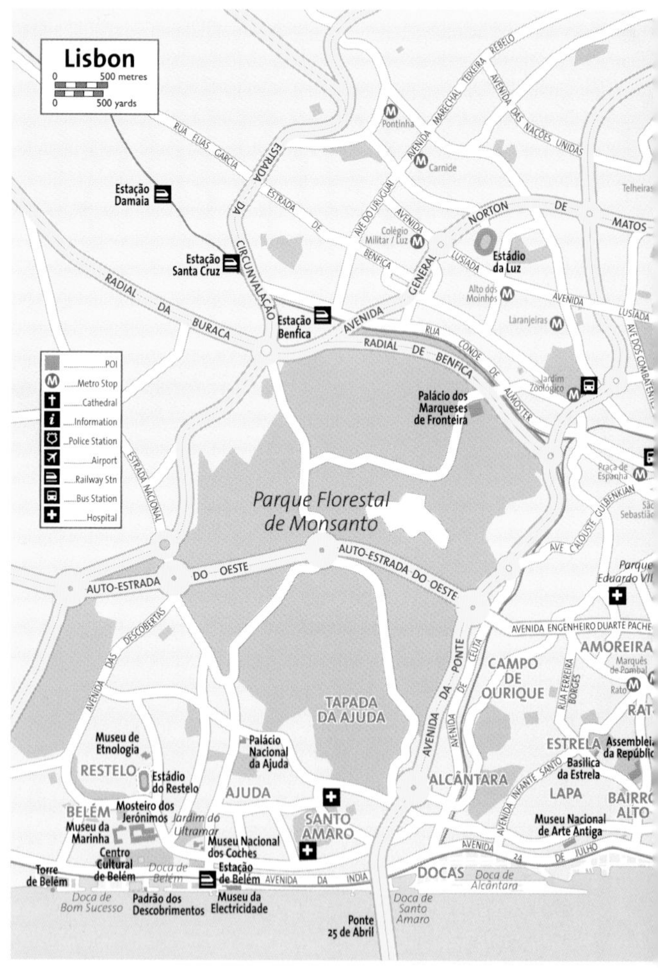
Lisbon
0 500 metres
0 500 yards
POI
Metro Stop
Cathedral
Information
Police Station
Airport
Railway Stn
Bus Station
Hospital
RUA ELIAS GARCIA
ESTRADA DA CIRCUNVALAÇÃO
ESTRADA DE BENFICA
AVENIDA MARECHAL TEIXEIRA REBELO
AVENIDA DAS NAÇÕES UNIDAS
Pontinha
Carnide
Telheiras
AVE DO URUGUAI
AVENIDA NORTON DE MATOS
Colégio Militar / Luz
Estádio da Luz
GENERAL
LUSÍADA
Alto dos Moinhos
AVENIDA LUSÍADA
Laranjeiras
Estação Damaia
Estação Santa Cruz
Estação Benfica
RADIAL DA BURACA
AVENIDA
RUA CONDE DE ALMOSTER
RADIAL DE BENFICA
Jardim Zoológico
AVE DOS COMBATENTES
Palácio dos Marqueses de Fronteira
Praça de Espanha
AVE CALOUSTE GULBENKIAN
ESTRADA NACIONAL
Parque Florestal de Monsanto
AUTO-ESTRADA DO OESTE
Parque Eduardo VII
AVENIDA ENGENHEIRO DUARTE PACHECO
AVENIDA DAS DESCOBERTAS
AVENIDA DA PONTE
AVENIDA DE CEUTA
CAMPO DE OURIQUE
RUA FERREIRA BORGES
AMOREIRAS
Marquês de Pombal
Rato
TAPADA DA AJUDA
Museu de Etnologia
Palácio Nacional da Ajuda
ESTRELA
Assembleia da República
RESTELO
Estádio do Restelo
ALCÂNTARA
AVENIDA INFANTE SANTO
Basílica da Estrela
AJUDA
LAPA
BAIRRO ALTO
BELÉM
Mosteiro dos Jerónimos
Jardim do Ultramar
Museu da Marinha
SANTO AMARO
Museu Nacional de Arte Antiga
Centro Cultural de Belém
Museu Nacional dos Coches
AVENIDA 24 DE JULHO
Torre de Belém
Doca de Belém
Estação de Belém
AVENIDA DA INDIA
DOCAS
Doca de Alcântara
Doca de Bom Sucesso
Padrão dos Descobrimentos
Museu da Electricidade
Doca de Santo Amaro
Ponte 25 de Abril

Ponte Vasco da Gama
Lumiar
Quinta das Conchas
Aeroporto de Portela
AVENIDA CIDADE DO PORTO
AVENIDA DOUTOR ALFREDO BENSAUDE
DOM HENRIQUE
Torre Vasco da Gama
Parque das Nações
Campo Grande
AVENIDA MARECHAL CRAVEIRO LOPES
AVENIDA DE BERLIM
Estação do Oriente
Pavilhão Atlântico
Oriente
INFANTE
AVENIDA DO BRASIL
AVENIDA MARECHAL GOMES DA COSTA
Doca dos Olivais
CAMPO GRANDE
Alvalade
Olivais
Cabo Ruivo
Oceanário
Cidade Universitária
Entre Campos
Estádio Primeiro de Maio
AVENIDA ALMIRANTE
CONDESTÁVEL
SANTO
Chelas
AVENIDA DE ROMA
Roma
Parque da Bela Vista
AVENIDA DOS ESTADOS UNIDOS DA AMÉRICA
AVENIDA INFANTE DOM HENRIQUE
REPUBLICA
Campo Pequeno
Areeiro
Bela Vista
Museu Calouste Gulbenkian
AVENIDA JOÃO XXI
CAMPO PEQUENO
ALMIRA
RUA CINTURA DO PORTO
Alameda
Olaias
SALDANHA
Saldanha
Picoas
Parque
RUA MORAIS SOARES
Arroios
REIS
Marquês de Pombal
Anjos
Intendente
AVE DA LIBERDADE
Avenida
GRAÇA
Rio Tejo
Coliseu dos Recreios
Martim Moniz
MOURARIA
Estação Santa Apolónia
Restauradores
Teatro Nacional Dona Maria II
Castelo de São Jorge
Rossio
BAIXA
ALFAMA
Santa Apolónia
CHIADO
Baixa-Chiado
Casa dos Bicos
Casa do Fado
Cais do Sodré
Sé Catedral
PRAÇA DO COMÉRCIO
Estação Cais do Sodré
Doca do Jardim do Tabaco
Doca da Marinha
Cais das Colunas
N

By water

Cacilheiros (small ferries) are used often here by locals travelling to and from work on the south side of the Tagus. The main ferry route is from Terreiro do Paço across the river, but tourist boats also operate between here and Parque das Nações (see page 110). For more information, see Transejo Ⓦ www.transtejo.pt

FINDING YOUR FEET

You'll need a map to find your way through some areas of the city, but don't panic if you do feel lost as it will not be long before you will find a viewing point and be able to reorientate yourself. Lisbon's *bairros* (neighbourhoods) have distinct characteristics.

While Portugal's crime rate is lower than in some countries, tourists are often targeted by opportunists. There has been a rise in the number of pickpockets in the past decade, particularly on tram no. 28. Also avoid walking home through dark streets of the Alfama and Bairro Alto late at night. You can always ask for a taxi from a bar or restaurant to your hotel.

ORIENTATION

Lisbon lies on the northeast bank of the mouth of the River Tagus and is built on seven hills: Castelo, Estrela, Graça, Monte, Penha de França, São Pedro de Alcântara and Santa Catarina. It's better known by its *bairros*. The easiest place to start is the Baixa, easily navigable because of its grid-like structure, starting from the Praça do Comércio on the riverside north of Rossio Square.

To the east of the Baixa is the Alfama, recognisable by its tangle of streets and crowned by the Castelo de São Jorge (see page 74). Beyond Alfama is the traditional neighbourhood of Graça, which boasts fabulous views of the city, and next door is Santa Apolónia on the riverside, the location of one of the major train stations. Further

TRAVEL CARD/LISBOA CARD

The **Lisboa Card**, available from tourist information outlets, gives free access to public transport, 26 museums, monuments and discounts at a large number of other attractions. A one-day card costs €14.85; two-day cards €25.50; three-day cards €31. If you don't want to be tied to seeing the attractions but would like to have the freedom of getting around the city, then you can also buy one-day passes in the metro. The **7 Colinas** rechargeable card lets you ride the buses, trams and metro.

northeast lie the Parque das Nações (see page 110) and the Vasco da Gama Bridge.

North of the Baixa and Rossio Square, the Avenida da Liberdade leads up to Praça Marquês de Pombal, a large roundabout with the Parque Eduardo VII to the north (see page 87). The main business areas of the city are located west and north of Pombal.

To the west of the Baixa are the lively old artistic districts of the Chiado and the Bairro Alto, and beyond lie the residential enclaves of Estrela and Madragoa. West along the river is the renovated dock area of Alcântara and the 25 de Abril Bridge, from where you can see the towering Cristo Rei (Christ the Redeemer) statue (although it is a miniature of the one in Rio de Janeiro). Westwards from the bridge is the historic area of Belém and the coastal road out of Lisbon to Cascais and Estoril.

GETTING AROUND

You will probably need to use the city's public transport system at some point, as Lisbon is both hilly and spread out. There is a comprehensive

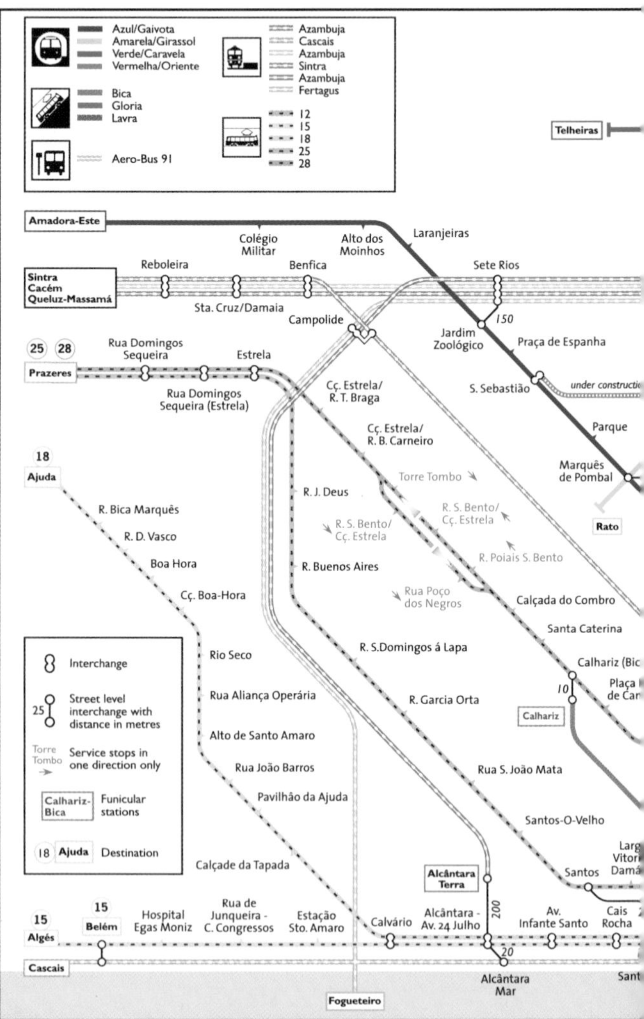

Azul/Gaivota
Amarela/Girassol
Verde/Caravela
Vermelha/Oriente
Bica
Gloria
Lavra
Aero-Bus 91
Azambuja
Cascais
Azambuja
Sintra
Azambuja
Fertagus
12
15
18
25
28
Telheiras
Amadora-Este
Colégio Militar
Alto dos Moinhos
Laranjeiras
Reboleira
Benfica
Sete Rios
Sintra
Cacém
Queluz-Massamá
Sta. Cruz/Damaia
Campolide
150
Jardim Zoológico
Praça de Espanha
25
28
Rua Domingos Sequeira
Estrela
Prazeres
Rua Domingos Sequeira (Estrela)
Cç. Estrela/ R. T. Braga
S. Sebastião
under constructi
Parque
Cç. Estrela/ R. B. Carneiro
18
Ajuda
Torre Tombo
Marquês de Pombal
R. J. Deus
R. Bica Marquês
R. S. Bento/ Cç. Estrela
R. S. Bento/ Cç. Estrela
Rato
R. D. Vasco
Boa Hora
R. Buenos Aires
R. Poiais S. Bento
Cç. Boa-Hora
Rua Poço dos Negros
Calçada do Combro
Santa Caterina
Rio Seco
R. S.Domingos á Lapa
Calhariz (Bic
Interchange
Street level interchange with distance in metres
25
10
Rua Aliança Operária
R. Garcia Orta
Calhariz
Alto de Santo Amaro
Torre Tombo
Service stops in one direction only
Rua João Barros
Rua S. João Mata
Calhariz-Bica
Funicular stations
Pavilhão da Ajuda
Santos-O-Velho
18
Ajuda
Destination
Calçade da Tapada
Alcântara Terra
Santos
15
Belém
15
Algés
Hospital Egas Moniz
Rua de Junqueira - C. Congressos
Estação Sto. Amaro
Calvário
Alcântara - Av. 24 Julho
200
Av. Infante Santo
Cais Rocha
20
Cascais
Alcântara Mar
Fogueteiro

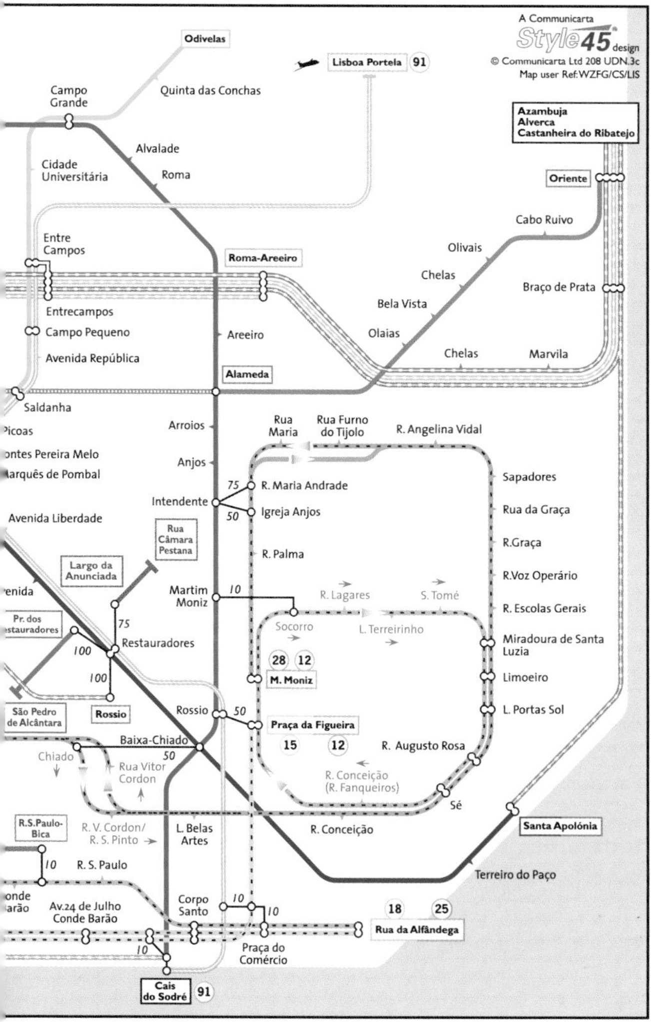

A Communicarta Style 45 design
© Communicarta Ltd 208 UDN.3c
Map user Ref: WZFG/CS/LIS

Odivelas
Lisboa Portela 91
Campo Grande
Quinta das Conchas
Azambuja
Alverca
Castanheira do Ribatejo
Alvalade
Cidade Universitária
Roma
Oriente
Cabo Ruivo
Entre Campos
Olivais
Roma-Areeiro
Chelas
Braço de Prata
Bela Vista
Entrecampos
Campo Pequeno
Areeiro
Olaias
Avenida República
Chelas
Marvila
Alameda
Saldanha
Picoas
Arroios
Rua Maria
Rua Furno do Tijolo
R. Angelina Vidal
Fontes Pereira Melo
Marquês de Pombal
Anjos
Sapadores
75
R. Maria Andrade
Intendente
Igreja Anjos
50
Rua da Graça
Avenida Liberdade
Rua Câmara Pestana
R.Graça
R. Palma
Largo da Anunciada
R.Voz Operário
Avenida
Martim Moniz
10
R. Lagares
S. Tomé
R. Escolas Gerais
Pr. dos Restauradores
75
Socorro
L. Terreirinho
Miradoura de Santa Luzia
Restauradores
100
28 12
100
M. Moniz
Limoeiro
Rossio
L. Portas Sol
São Pedro de Alcântara
Rossio
50
Praça da Figueira
Baixa-Chiado
15 12
R. Augusto Rosa
Chiado
50
Rua Vitor Cordon
R. Conceição (R. Fanqueiros)
Sé
R.S.Paulo-Bica
R. V. Cordon/ R. S. Pinto
L. Belas Artes
R. Conceição
Santa Apolónia
10
R. S. Paulo
Terreiro do Paço
Conde Barão
Av.24 de Julho Conde Barão
Corpo Santo
10
10
18 25
Rua da Alfândega
10
Praça do Comércio
Cais do Sodré 91

city bus service in Lisbon run by **Carris** (Ⓦ www.carris.pt) and night buses run from Cais do Sodré (see page 48) through the main areas of the city. Tickets can be bought from the driver but it's cheaper to buy multiples or passes for a day or longer. Trams and funiculars are also a good option, depending on where you are going. The old tram no. 28 is a good way of ascending to Castelo de São Jorge in Alfama, and also travels between Ourique and Graça via Estrela, Bairro Alto and Baixa. Modern tram no. 15 is the best way of getting to Belém from the old city and leaves from Praça do Comércio.

Lisbon's metro system (Ⓦ www.metrolisboa.pt) covers a wide expanse of city. As with the buses and trams, it may be worth buying a Lisboa Card for a day or more (see page 53).

Please note that where no public transport is given in particular listings in this guide, it means that there is no station or stop nearby, and you should consider walking or taking a taxi.

CAR HIRE

Driving is only the best option if you're planning on exploring some out-of-town places. Car hire in Portugal can be reasonable compared with other countries in Western Europe, but for the best rates it's better to book in advance. Several companies operate at the airport, including:

Auto Jardim Ⓣ (21) 846 2916 Ⓦ www.auto-jardim.com
Avis Ⓣ (21) 843 5550 Ⓦ www.avis.com.pt
Budget Ⓣ (21) 994 2402 Ⓦ www.budgetportugal.com
Europcar Ⓣ (21) 840 1176 Ⓦ www.europcar.com
Guerin Ⓣ (21) 848 6191 Ⓦ www.guerin.pt
Hertz Ⓣ (21) 843 8660 Ⓦ www.hertz.co.uk
Sixt Ⓣ (21) 799 8701 Ⓦ www.sixt.pt

Azulejo *tiles cover many façades in Lisbon*

THE CITY OF Lisbon

The Baixa, Chiado & Bairro Alto

Part of the traditional old centre of the city and still very much a focal point for tourists, the Baixa, Chiado and Bairro Alto are visually quite distinct from the rest of Lisbon. Following the destruction of much of the area by the Great Earthquake of 1755, the Baixa (or Baixa Pombalina) was rebuilt by the Marquês de Pombal, who gave it the grid-like structure that can still be seen today. The streets are named after the traders and craftsmen based here since the Age of Discoveries. In the Bairro Alto, the ruins of the Convento do Carmo are testament to the earthquake's ferocity, but the area certainly isn't depressed by it. Along with the elegant Chiado, the more bohemian Bairro Alto is cosmopolitan and renowned for its artistic and literary connections, as well as the numerous *fado* houses, restaurants and lively nightlife.

SIGHTS & ATTRACTIONS

The pleasant and airy Baixa is easy to navigate from Praça do Comércio to Rossio and is a great place to start exploring the city.

Ascensor da Bica (Bica Funicular)

Descending from the edge of Bairro Alto towards Cais do Sodré through the scenic *bairro* of Bica, lined with funky bars and cafés, this funicular affords spectacular views of the Tagus below. ⓐ Largo do Calhariz – Rua de São Paulo ⓑ 07.00–21.00 Mon–Sat, 09.00–21.00 Sun ⓣ Metro: Baixa-Chiado; Tram: 28

Convento & Museu Arqueológico do Carmo (Carmo Convent & Archaeological Museum)

The skeletal ruins of this 14th-century convent church survived the

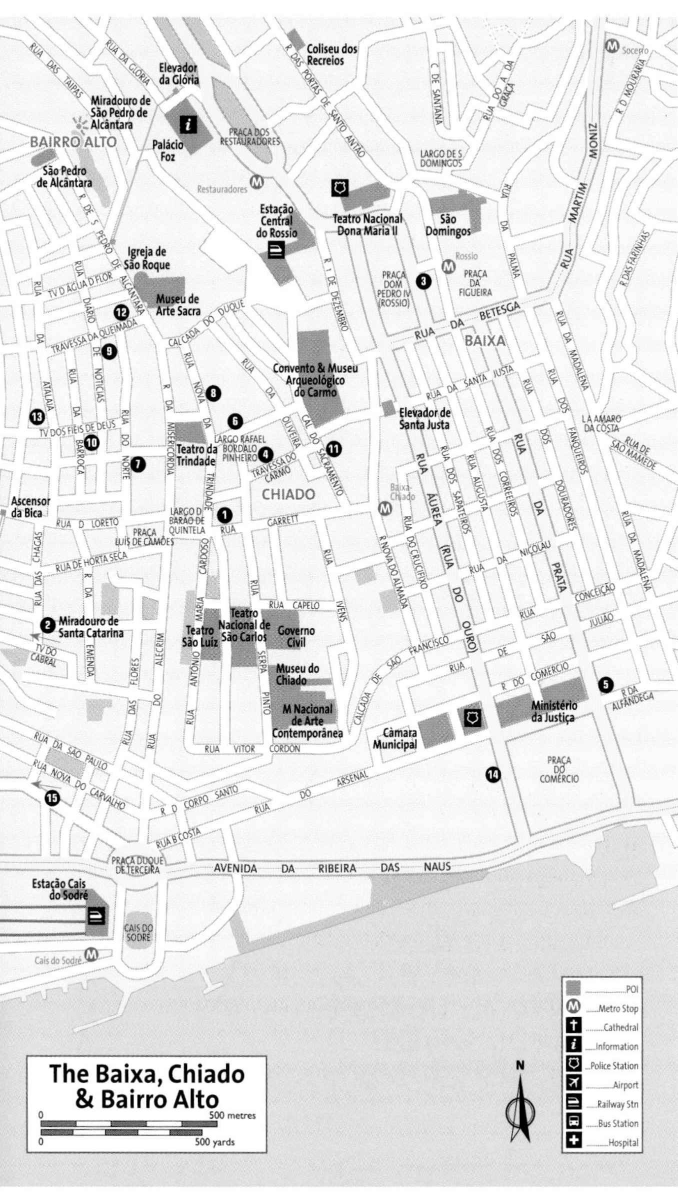

Coliseu dos Recreios
Elevador da Glória
Miradouro de São Pedro de Alcântara
BAIRRO ALTO
São Pedro de Alcântara
Palácio Foz
PRACA DOS RESTAURADORES
Restauradores
Estação Central do Rossio
Teatro Nacional Dona Maria II
São Domingos
LARGO DE S DOMINGOS
Rossio
PRAÇA DOM PEDRO IV (ROSSIO)
PRAÇA DA FIGUEIRA
Soceiro
Igreja de São Roque
Museu de Arte Sacra
Convento & Museu Arqueológico do Carmo
Elevador de Santa Justa
BAIXA
Teatro da Trindade
LARGO RAFAEL BORDALO PINHEIRO
CHIADO
Baixa-Chiado
Ascensor da Bica
LARGO D BARÃO DE QUINTELA
PRAÇA LUÍS DE CAMÕES
Miradouro de Santa Catarina
Teatro São Luíz
Teatro Nacional de São Carlos
Governo Civil
Museu do Chiado
M Nacional de Arte Contemporânea
Câmara Municipal
Ministério da Justiça
PRAÇA DO COMÉRCIO
PRAÇA DUQUE DE TERCEIRA
Estação Cais do Sodré
CAIS DO SODRÉ
Cais do Sodré
RUA DAS TAIPAS
RUA DA GLÓRIA
R DAS PORTAS DE SANTO ANTÃO
C DE SANTANA
RUA DO A DA GRAÇA
R D MOURARIA
RUA MARTIM MONIZ
RUA DA PALMA
R DAS FARINHAS
R DE S PEDRO DE ALCÂNTARA
TV D ÁGUA D FLOR
RUA DIÁRIO DE NOTÍCIAS
TRAVESSA DA QUEIMADA
CALÇADA DO DUQUE
RUA DA BETESGA
R 1 DE DEZEMBRO
RUA DA ATALAIA
RUA DA BARROCA
RUA DO NORTE
TV DOS FIÉIS DE DEUS
R DA MISERICÓRDIA
RUA NOVA DA TRINDADE
RUA DO CARMO
RUA DA OLIVEIRA
CAL DO SACRAMENTO
TRAVESSA DO CARMO
RUA DA SANTA JUSTA
RUA DA MADALENA
LA AMARO DA COSTA
RUA DE SÃO MAMEDE
RUA DOS FANQUEIROS
RUA DOS DOURADORES
RUA DA PRATA
RUA DOS CORREEIROS
RUA AUGUSTA
RUA DOS SAPATEIROS
RUA ÁUREA (RUA DO OURO)
RUA DO CRUCIFIXO
R NOVA DO ALMADA
RUA GARRETT
RUA IVENS
RUA CAPELO
RUA DE NICOLAU
RUA DA CONCEIÇÃO
RUA DE SÃO JULIÃO
R DO COMÉRCIO
R DA ALFÂNDEGA
CALÇADA DE SÃO FRANCISCO
RUA D LORETO
RUA DAS CHAGAS
RUA DE HORTA SECA
R DA EMENDA
TV DO CABRAL
RUA DAS FLORES
RUA DO ALECRIM
RUA ANTÓNIO MARIA CARDOSO
RUA SERPA PINTO
RUA VITOR CORDON
RUA DA SÃO PAULO
RUA NOVA DO CARVALHO
R D CORPO SANTO
RUA DO ARSENAL
RUA B COSTA
AVENIDA DA RIBEIRA DAS NAUS
The Baixa, Chiado & Bairro Alto
0
500 metres
0
500 yards
N
POI
Metro Stop
Cathedral
Information
Police Station
Airport
Railway Stn
Bus Station
Hospital

1755 earthquake. The archaeological museum that occupies the site today has an interesting collection of artefacts dating back to the Visigoths and Romans, as well as pieces found in the Americas. ⓐ Largo do Carmo ⓣ (21) 347 08629 ⓑ 10.00–18.00 May–Sept; until 17.00 Oct–Apr ⓝ Metro: Baixa-Chiado; Tram: 28; Lift: Elevador de Santa Justa

Elevador da Glória

One of the funiculars built to cope with Lisbon's hills, the Elevador da Glória links Restauradores with the Bairro Alto and the Miradouro de São Pedro de Alcântara. It's just a short ride but a steep uphill walk, especially after a day's sightseeing. ⓐ São Pedro de Alcântara – Restauradores ⓑ 07.00–00.00 Mon–Thur, 07.00–00.30 Fri & Sat, 09.00–00.00 Sun ⓝ Metro: Restauradores

Elevador de Santa Justa

At the junction of Rua do Ouro and Rua da Santa Justa, the Elevador de Santa Justa is a dazzling iron structure. It links the Baixa with Bairro Alto and has a viewing tower and café at the top. ⓐ Largo do Carmo – Rua do Ouro ⓑ 07.00–21.00 (winter); 07.00–23.00 (summer) ⓝ Metro: Baixa-Chiado; Tram: 28

Igreja de São Roque

Initially constructed in the 16th century, this church was altered over the next few centuries, including the addition of the Chapel of São João (St John). Look out for the different artistic styles, such as the 16th-century *azulejos*, the *trompe-l'oeil* ceiling and paintings by Italian artists. ⓐ Largo Trindade Coelho ⓣ (21) 323 5381 ⓑ 08.30–17.00 Mon–Fri, 09.30–17.00 Sat & Sun ⓝ Metro: Restauradores; Lift: Elevador da Glória

---

Beautiful city views from the Elevador de Santa Justa

A view uphill – Rua do Alecrim

Miradouro de Santa Catarina

Further on from the Praça Luís de Camões towards Estrela, the Santa Catarina viewing point is set in a green, tree-lined square. Ⓐ Travessa de Santa Catarina Ⓣ Tram: 28

Miradouro de São Pedro de Alcântara

At the top of the Elevador da Glória is one of the most pleasant viewing points in the city. Ⓐ São Pedro de Alcântara Ⓣ Metro: Restauradores; Lift: Elevador da Glória

Praça do Comércio

Located at the south entrance to the Baixa, locals sometimes call this wide-open square by its old name, Terreiro do Paço, because of the Paços da Ribeira royal palace that stood here before the earthquake of 1755. It also has the nickname of Black Horse Square, due to the bronze statue of Dom José I (king at that time) that stands in the centre. You'll find the Lisbon Welcome Centre here. Ⓣ Metro: Baixa-Chiado; Tram: 15

Praça Luís de Camões

This small square is dedicated to one of Portugal's most renowned poets, Luís de Camões, author of *The Lusiads* (1572), whose narrative follows the journey of Vasco da Gama. At the centre of the square is a large bronze statue of Camões. Ⓣ Tram: 28

Rossio & Praça da Figueira

At the northern end of the Baixa Pombalina is the Praça da Figueira, a plain Pombaline square with a statue of Dom João I at the centre. It's a good place to stop for coffee and cake. To the left is Praça Dom Pedro IV, whose statue is also at the centre. However, it's more

FERNANDO PESSOA
Born in Lisbon in 1888, Fernando Pessoa is Portugal's most celebrated poet. He believed texts should be appreciated for themselves and not for the author, and so began to write under pseudonyms (as himself) and heteronyms (as an alter-ego). Much of his work remained unpublished until after his death in 1935. Lisbon was at the heart of his writing, including his major prose works, *The Book of Disquietude*, and *Lisbon: What the Tourist Should See* (1992). Other notable works include *Poesías de Alvaro Campos* (1944), *Odes to Ricardo Reis* (1946) and *Cartas de Amor* (1988).

commonly known as Rossio Square, after the train station on the left-hand side. Ⓝ Metro: Rossio

CULTURE

Museu do Chiado

This former traditionalist museum was redesigned in 1994 by Jean-Michel Wilmotte. With neo-modern architecture of suspended walkways, floors and ceilings, the museum hosts temporary exhibitions and showcases an impressive collection of paintings, sculptures and drawings spanning 1850 to 1960. ⓐ Rua Serpa Pinto 4 ⓣ (21) 3432 148 ◷ 10.00–18.00 Tues–Sun, closed Mon ⓦ www.museudochiado-ipmuseus.pt Ⓝ Metro: Baixa-Chiado; Tram: 28

Teatro Nacional Dona Maria II

The Teatro Nacional Dona Maria II was originally built in the 1840s by Italian architect Fortunato Lodi in a neoclassical style. It offers

Pessoa sits outside a café in Bairro Alto

guided tours and a programme of theatre, circus and performance art. Praça Dom Pedro IV (21) 3250 835 www.teatro-dmaria.pt Metro: Rossio

Teatro Nacional de São Carlos

Located in the Chiado, the theatre was built in the 18th century as a replacement for the opera house that once stood here, and includes a neoclassical façade and elaborate rococo interior. It hosts a busy programme of opera, classical music and theatre. ⓐ Rua Serpa Pinto 9 ⓣ (21) 3253 045 ⓦ www.saocarlos.pt ⓝ Metro: Baixa-Chiado; Tram: 28

Teatro São Luíz

Opened in 1894, this theatre was once frequented by the 'elegant classes' of the era. Today it presents a diverse range of dance, theatre and music. ⓐ Rua António Maria Cardoso 38 ⓣ (21) 3257 650 ⓦ www.teatrosaoluiz.egeac.pt ⓝ Metro: Baixa-Chiado; Tram: 28

RETAIL THERAPY

The Baixa is one of the most traditional and pleasant shopping areas in the city with international chains as well as a few local stores selling leather goods and jewellery. Look out for the names of the streets, which reflect the traders and craftsmen that worked here for hundreds of years. In the Praça do Comércio you'll also find a parade of shops, including some local crafts. Just round the corner in the renovated Chiado there are trendy clothes shops and large bookstores such as FNAC inside the **Armazéns do Chiado** shopping centre (ⓦ www.armazensdochiado.com). High-profile Portuguese fashion designers have their flagship stores in the Chiado-Bairro Alto area. Look out for creations by **Ana Salazar** (ⓐ Rua do Carmo 87 ⓦ www.anasalazar.pt) and **Fátima Lopes** (ⓐ Rua da Atalaia 36 ⓦ www.fatima-lopes.com).

TAKING A BREAK

The Baixa, Bairro Alto and Chiado are all renowned for being hangouts of artistic types, particularly the Cais do Sodré area.

A Brasileira (do Chiado) ££ ❶ This popular café is a must. ⓐ Rua Garrett 100–122 ⓣ (21) 3469 541 ⓦ www.abrasileira.pt ⓛ 08.00–02.00 ⓜ Metro: Baixa-Chiado

Noobai Café ££ ❷ Sip a health juice or an exotic tea while taking in splendid city views at this charming café. The light Mediterranean fare is worth a try, too. ⓐ Miradouro de Santa Catarina ⓣ (21) 346 5014 ⓦ www.noobaicafe.com ⓛ 12.00–00.00 ⓜ Metro: Baixa-Chiado

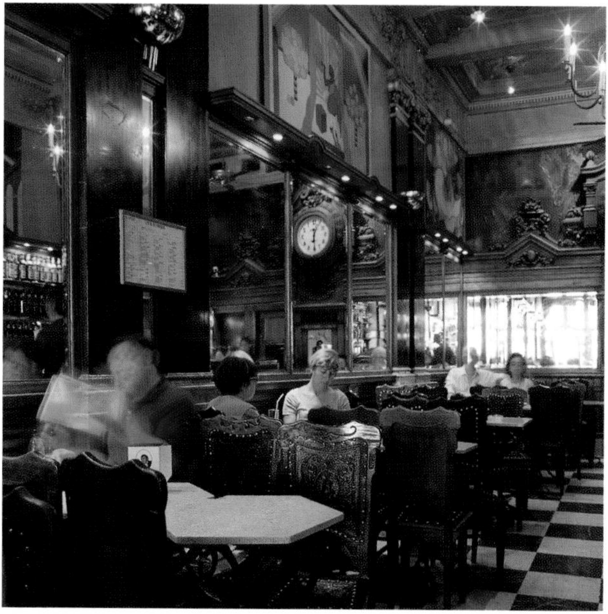

A Brasileira is an authentic Portuguese café

Baixa's main street, Rua Augusta, has plenty of restaurants

Pastelaria Suiça ££ ❸ Great outdoor seating, and its cakes are considered some of the best in Lisbon. ⓐ Praça Dom Pedro IV 96–104 ⓣ (21) 321 4090 ⓒ 07.00–21.30 ⓦ www.casasuica.pt ⓜ Metro: Rossio

Vertigo Café ££ ❹ This popular hangout with a retro vibe has a great selection of teas and delicious snacks. ⓐ Travessa do Carmo 4 ⓣ (21) 343 3112 ⓒ 10.00–00.00 ⓜ Metro: Baixa-Chiado

Café Martinho da Arcada £££ ❺ It can be crowded with tourists, but stick with it for the food. ⓐ Praça do Comércio 7 ⓣ (21) 887 9259 ⓒ 07.30–22.00 Mon–Sat, closed Sun ⓜ Metro: Baixa-Chiado

Royale Café £££ ❻ This elegant Chiado spot serves great organic treats and a nice offering of coffees and teas. ⓐ Largo Rafael Bordalo Pinheiro 29 ⓣ (21) 346 9125 ⓦ www.royalecafe.com ⓛ 10.00–00.00 Mon–Sat, 10.00–20.00 Sun ⓜ Metro: Baixa-Chiado

AFTER DARK

The Bairro Alto has long been a favourite for eating, drinking and dancing in Lisbon.

RESTAURANTS & FADO HOUSES

Cantinho do Bem Estar £ ❼ This tiny storefront restaurant serves tasty portions of Portuguese mainstays. ⓐ Rua do Norte 46 ⓣ (21) 346 4265 ⓛ 12.30–14.30, 19.30–22.45 Tues–Sat, 19.30–22.45 Sun, closed Mon ⓜ Metro: Baixa-Chiado

Cervejaria Trindade £ ❽ Relaxed and friendly, it's great for steaks and seafood. ⓐ Rua Nova da Trindade 20 ⓣ (21) 342 3506 ⓦ www.cervejariatrindade.pt ⓛ 10.00–02.00 ⓜ Metro: Baixa-Chiado

Adega Mesquita ££ ❾ Traditional but restored *fado* house that serves up tasty Portuguese cuisine. Choose from a menu of kid, cod, squid, rabbit and beef. ⓐ Rua Diário de Noticias 107 ⓣ (21) 321 9280 ⓦ www.adegamesquita.com ⓛ 20.00–02.00 Mon–Sat, closed Sun ⓜ Metro: Baixa-Chiado

Arcadas do Faia ££ ❿ *Fado* house renowned for its authentic but expensive cuisine. ⓐ Rua da Barroca 54–56 ⓣ (21) 342 6742 ⓦ www.ofaia.com ⓛ 20.00–02.00 Mon–Sat, closed Sun ⓜ Metro: Baixa-Chiado

Sacramento ££ ⓫ This swanky restaurant features modern versions of Portuguese classics. ⓐ Calçada do Sacramento 40–46 ⓣ (21) 342 0572 ⓦ www.sacramentodochiado.com ◷ 12.00–15.00, 19.30–00.00 Mon–Fri, 19.30–00.00 Sat & Sun ⓜ Metro: Baixa-Chiado

Café Luso £££ ⓬ One of Lisbon's oldest *fado* houses, dating back to 1927, this basement venue has a restaurant and a nightly performance by a local folk group. ⓐ Travessa da Queimada 10 ⓣ (21) 342 2281 ⓦ www.cafeluso.pt ◷ 19.30–02.00 ⓜ Metro: Baixa-Chiado

Pap' Açorda £££ ⓭ One of Lisbon's most famous restaurants. Have a drink at the marble-topped bar before enjoying the menu from the Alentejo region, particularly shellfish. ⓐ Rua da Atalaia 57–59 ⓣ (21) 346 4811 ◷ 12.30–14.30, 20.00–23.00 Tues–Sat, closed Sun & Mon ⓜ Metro: Baixa-Chiado

Terreiro do Paço £££ ⓮ A sleek purveyor of updated local recipes. ⓐ Lisbon Welcome Centre, Praça do Comércio ⓣ (21) 031 2850 ⓦ www.terreiropaco.com ◷ 12.30–15.00, 20.00–23.00 Mon–Fri, 20.00–23.00 Sat, closed Sun ⓜ Metro: Rossio

Yasmin £££ ⓯ Creative fusion cuisine served in a beautifully designed space close to the waterfront in the Cais do Sodré area below Bica. ⓐ Rua da Moeda 1A ⓣ (21) 393 0074 ⓦ www.yasmin-lx.com ◷ 19.30–24.30 ⓜ Metro: Cais do Sodré

BARS & CLUBS

Bicaense A fun bar in Bica that's a boho hangout, with a small dance floor and excellent cocktails. ⓐ Rua da Bica Duarte Belo 42 ◷ 20.00–02.00 Mon–Sat, closed Sun ⓜ Metro: Rossio

Capela Housed in a former chapel, this bar/club is usually packed and plays electronic, dub and groove. Ⓐ Rua da Atalaia 45 Ⓣ (21) 347 0072 Ⓛ 22.00–04.00 Mon–Sat, closed Sun Ⓜ Metro: Baixa-Chiado

Clandestino This graffiti-covered bar is a Bairro Alto old-timer, still going strong. Ⓐ Rua da Barroca 99 Ⓣ (21) 346 8194 Ⓛ 22.00–04.00 Mon–Sat, closed Sun Ⓜ Metro: Baixa-Chiado

Clube da Esquina A laid-back corner bar with a DJ most nights. Ⓐ Rua da Barroca 30 Ⓛ 21.30–02.00 Ⓜ Metro: Baixa-Chiado

Frágil Classic club that plays a mix of dance music, reggae, samba and drum 'n' bass. Ⓐ Rua da Atalaia 126 Ⓣ (21) 346 9578 Ⓛ 23.30–04.00 Ⓜ Metro: Baixa-Chiado

Ginjinha do Rossio A tiny bar that serves nothing but shots of *ginjinha* (a cherry-like fruit liqueur). Ⓐ Largo São Domingos 8 Ⓛ 09.00–22.30 Ⓜ Metro: Restauradores

Majong This avant garde Bairro Alto bar is a gathering spot of the upwardly mobile artsy crowd. Ⓐ Rua da Atalaia 3 Ⓛ 21.30–04.00 Ⓜ Metro: Baixa-Chiado

Pavilhão Chinês One of Lisbon's most atmospheric bars. Ⓐ Rua Dom Pedro V 89 Ⓣ (21) 342 4729 Ⓛ 18.00–02.00 Mon–Sat, 21.00–02.00 Sun Ⓜ Metro: Restauradores

Solar do Vinho do Porto Sink into the comfy armchairs and select from 300 varieties of port. Ⓐ Rua de São Pedro de Alcântara 45 Ⓣ (21) 347 5707 Ⓛ 11.00–00.00 Mon–Sat, closed Sun Ⓜ Metro: Restauradores

Alfama & Graça

The Alfama is the oldest district in Lisbon, a clutch of ancient houses, churches, squares and narrow cobbled streets that clings to the hillside just east of the Baixa and sweeps down to the Tagus. It was the Moors that built the first fortified settlement in the city – the Castelo de São Jorge (see page 74) that crowns the Alfama. The Moors were driven away by Dom Afonso Henriques in 1147, and the district became home to royals and the aristocracy. Once they left, the Alfama fell into decline and has remained an area of patchwork buildings. Apart from the castle, the district miraculously survived the 1755 earthquake, though the poverty remained.

SIGHTS & ATTRACTIONS

The easiest way to access the Alfama is by jumping on a no. 28 tram to the top of the hill. From there it's just a short stroll up to the Castelo de São Jorge. After your castle visit it's all downhill in the best possible sense, past the Museu de Artes Decorativas, the Santa Luzia viewing point and the Sé Catedral, through the old Jewish quarter and down to the Casa dos Bicos near the riverfront. If you circle round to the far side of the castle you can visit the Miradouro de Graça and then the Mosteiro de São Vicente de Fora and the Panteão Nacional.

Igreja da Conceição Velha

If you are walking back towards the Baixa after seeing the Casa dos Bicos, take a look at the doorway of this church. Built on the grounds of a former Jewish synagogue in the 16th century, the church was damaged, like so many buildings, in 1755. What survived and is most notable is the Manueline portal. Look out for the elaborate symbols of

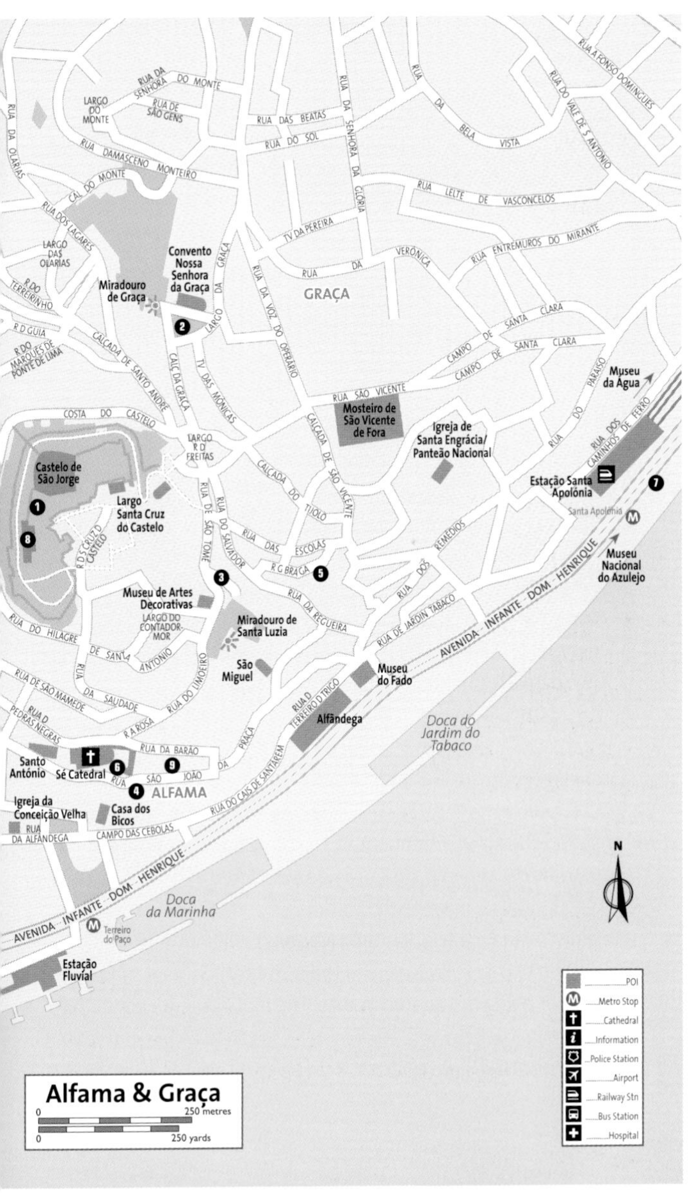

Alfama & Graça
0
250 metres
0
250 yards
GRAÇA
ALFAMA
Castelo de São Jorge
Largo Santa Cruz do Castelo
Miradouro de Graça
Convento Nossa Senhora da Graça
Mosteiro de São Vicente de Fora
Igreja de Santa Engrácia/ Panteão Nacional
Estação Santa Apolónia
Santa Apolónia
Museu da Água
Museu Nacional do Azulejo
Museu de Artes Decorativas
Miradouro de Santa Luzia
São Miguel
Museu do Fado
Alfândega
Doca do Jardim do Tabaco
Santo António
Sé Catedral
Igreja da Conceição Velha
Casa dos Bicos
Doca da Marinha
Terreiro do Paço
Estação Fluvial
N
POI
Metro Stop
Cathedral
Information
Police Station
Airport
Railway Stn
Bus Station
Hospital

CASTELO DE SÃO JORGE (CASTLE OF ST GEORGE)

One of the most prominent testaments to the city's history, the existing battlements of the castle were built by the Moors. When they were expelled, the castle became a royal residence, undergoing various additions, alterations and renovations. Partially destroyed by successive earthquakes, particularly the great one of 1755, it was classified as a National Monument in 1910 and underwent restoration in the 1940s and 1990s. Surrounded by a dry moat, it features a statue of St George at the entrance. Inside the first square, the Praça de Armas, look out for the statue of Afonso Henriques, the first king of Portugal, and take in the panoramic views of the city (take time to look at the *azulejos*, which give you an idea of what you are seeing). Ⓐ Castelo de São Jorge Ⓣ (21) 880 0620 Ⓦ www.castelosaojorge.egeac.pt 🕒 09.00–21.00 Mar–Oct; 09.00–18.00 Nov–Feb Ⓣ Tram: 28, 18, 12; Bus: 37. Admission charge

state, religion, nature and discovery that characterise this architectural style, including the Portuguese coat of arms, the Cross of the Order of Christ and the armillary sphere. Ⓐ Rua da Alfândega Ⓣ (21) 887 0202 🕒 09.00–17.00 Mon–Fri, 09.00–13.00 Sat, closed Sun Ⓣ Tram: 18, 25

Igreja de Santa Engrácia/Panteão Nacional

The church was first built here in the 16th century, but was knocked down after being desecrated in 1630. The replacement church then

◐ *Dom Afonso Henriques stands tall at the top of the hill*

Castelo de São Jorge – the crown jewel of the Alfama district

collapsed after storm damage in 1681. Construction of the replacement wasn't completed until the mid-20th century. The octagonal structure, baroque figurines and main church were designed by architect João Atunes. The dome was added in the 1960s and it was declared the National Pantheon in 1916. Today you can see cenotaphs dedicated to

Afonso de Albuquerque (first viceroy of Portuguese India), Henry the Navigator, Vasco da Gama, Pedro Alvares de Cabral (who discovered Brazil), Nuno Alveres Pereira (who secured Portugal's independence from Spain) and Luís de Camões (see page 63). Ⓐ Campo de Santa Clara Ⓣ (21) 885 4820 Ⓛ 10.00–17.00 Tues–Sun, closed Mon Ⓝ Bus: 35, 781, 782; Tram: 28

Miradouro de Graça

This viewing point in Graça, on one of Lisbon's highest hills, offers one of the best panoramas in the city. Lined with pine trees, it is a relaxing and romantic spot with views of the castle behind and the city in front. There is also a café here, so you can stop for a rest (see page 81). Ⓐ Largo da Graça, off Calçada da Graça Ⓝ Tram: 28; Bus: 34

Miradouro de Santa Luzia

This viewing point is recognisable because of both the Santa Luzia Church and the tiled panel depicting Lisbon before the 1755 earthquake. A great place for a breather if it is sunny; if you are walking downhill, go down the steps on the far side of the church (Beco da Corvinha) – here you will see the remains of Moorish walls. Ⓐ Rua do Limoeiro Ⓝ Tram: 28

Mosteiro de São Vicente de Fora

Built in the 16th and 17th centuries, and partially damaged in 1755, the church is named after Lisbon's patron saint. You can easily spot its Italian façade and two white towers from the viewing points at the top of the Alfama. The real highlight are the cloisters; added in the 18th century, they are decorated with elaborate *azulejos*. Ⓐ Rua de São Vicente Ⓣ (21) 882 4400 Ⓛ 09.00–12.30, 15.00–18.00 Ⓝ Tram: 28; Bus: 34

Sé Catedral

After liberating the city in the 12th century, Portugal's Conquistador and first king, Afonso Henriques, ordered that the cathedral should be built. A mixture of Gothic and Romanesque styles, it didn't come out unscathed from the 1755 earthquake. It was renovated and today you can go inside and visit its small museum. ⓐ Largo da Sé ⓣ (21) 887 6628 Ⓛ Church 09.00–19.00, Museum 10.00–13.00, 14.00–17.00 Mon–Sat, closed Sun Ⓝ Tram: 18, 25; Bus: 37

CULTURE

Museu da Água (Water Museum)

Housed inside the former boiler room, the permanent exhibit of this water museum traces the evolution of Lisbon's water supply from the Roman era until today. ⓐ Rua do Alviela 12, Santa Apolónia ⓣ (21) 810 0215 Ⓛ 10.00–18.00 Mon–Sat, closed Sun Ⓝ Bus: 35, 12, 706, 794. Admission charge

Museu de Artes Decorativas (Museum of Decorative Arts)

Housed in a former 17th-century palace, both the building and the collection were donated by banker and art collector Ricardo do Espírito Silva to the Portuguese state. Inside you can see an example of a typical 18th-century aristocratic residence and an important collection of Portuguese tiles, furniture and textiles. ⓐ Largo das Portas do Sol 2 ⓣ (21) 881 4600, ⓦ www.fress.pt Ⓛ 10.00–17.00 Ⓝ Tram: 28, 12; Bus: 37. Admission charge

Museu do Fado (Fado Museum)

At the entrance to the Alfama, this museum and cultural centre dedicated to soulful *fado* features a permanent exhibition, temporary

You might be glad of a tram to climb Alfama's hills

shows, a store, a small auditorium and a café. The museum showcases a wealth of *fado*-related artefacts including a collection of Portuguese guitars by famous *fadistas*, sheet music, posters, stage props and old records. ⓐ Largo do Chafariz de Dentro 1 ⓣ (21) 882 3470 ⓦ www.museudofado.egeac.pt ⓗ 10.00–18.00 Tues–Sun, closed Mon ⓡ Bus: 35, 39, 46, 59. Admission charge

Museu Nacional do Azulejo (National Tile Museum)
Located east of the Alfama along the riverfront, this museum in a former convent has one of the most important collections of *azulejos* in the world. Dating from the 15th century to the present, the tiles reflect both the cultural and political history of the city and the country, from the early geometric patterns of the Moorish tiles to the modernist ones found in the metro station. ⓐ Rua da Madre de Deus 4 ⓣ (21) 810 0340 ⓦ www.mnazulejo-ipmuseus.pt ⓗ 10.00–18.00 Wed–Sun, 14.00–18.00 Tues, closed Mon ⓡ Bus: 718, 742. Admission charge

RETAIL THERAPY

The Alfama is not renowned for shopping, but if you like rummaging for a bargain then head to Feira da Ladra market, which takes place every Tuesday and Saturday. The market is an array of household goods, bric-a-brac and the occasional antique. Go early so you can grab the best bargains.

TAKING A BREAK

With so many fabulous views of the city, the Alfama is an ideal place to stop for some refreshment.

Café do Castelo de São Jorge £ ❶ Plenty of outdoor shaded seating. ⓐ Castelo de São Jorge ⓣ (21) 880 0620 ⓛ 09.00–21.00 Mar–Oct; 09.00–18.00 Nov–Feb ⓦ Tram: 28; Bus: 37

Café Esplanada da Graça £ ❷ Have a drink in the shade surrounded by pine trees, with a castle backdrop and views across to the Baixa and Bairro Alto. ⓐ Esplanada da Graça, off Calçada da Graça ⓛ 10.00–02.00 ⓦ Tram: 28; Bus: 37

Cerca Moura £ ❸ A favourite with locals, it offers great views over the Alfama rooftops to the Tagus. ⓐ Largo das Portas do Sol 4, off Rua de São Tomé ⓣ (21) 887 4859 ⓛ 10.00–02.00 ⓦ Tram: 28

Pois, Café £ ❹ A loungey Austrian-run café where it's easy to while away hours reading and sipping a coffee. ⓐ Rua São João da Praça 93–95 ⓣ (21) 886 2497 ⓛ 11.00–20.00 Tues–Sun, closed Mon ⓦ Tram: 12, 28

AFTER DARK

Although not the main area for clubbing and dining in Lisbon, this zone still offers some excellent options.

RESTAURANTS & FADO HOUSES

Dragão de Alfama £ ❺ Serves typical Portuguese food such as fried squid and plates of *presunto* (smoked ham). Live *fado* music every Thursday, Friday and Saturday. ⓐ Rua Guilherme Braga 8 (by Largo de Sto Estevão) ⓣ (21) 886 7737 ⓛ 08.00–00.00 ⓦ Metro: Martim Moniz

Viagem dos Sabores ££ ❻ Cosy restaurant near the cathedral, with a cosmopolitan menu of well-executed dishes from all corners of the world. ⓐ Rua São João da Praça 103 ⓣ (21) 887 0189 ⓒ 20.00–22.30 Mon–Thur, 20.00–23.30 Fri & Sat, closed Sun ⓝ Tram: 28, 12

Bica do Sapato £££ ❼ A warehouse conversion that attracts local celebrities. Overlooking the river, it serves Portuguese and international food and upstairs has a sushi bar. ⓐ Av. Infante Dom Henrique, Armazém B ⓣ (21) 881 0320 ⓦ www.bicadosapato.com ⓒ 12.30–14.30, 20.00–23.30 Tues–Sun, 20.00–23.30 Mon ⓝ Metro: Olaias

Casa do Leão £££ ❽ With its superb location in the grounds of the Castelo de São Jorge, this restaurant is perfect for intimate dinners, and has great views over the city. ⓐ Castelo de São Jorge ⓣ (21) 888 0154 ⓒ 12.00–15.00, 20.00–22.30 ⓝ Metro: Martim Moniz

Clube de Fado £££ ❾ This *fado* house is an old building with columns, arches and even a Moorish well in the corner. A very traditional way to enjoy good Portuguese food and hear some of the best *fado* in the area where it first emerged. ⓐ Rua São João da Praça 94 ⓣ (21) 885 2704 ⓦ www.clube-de-fado.com ⓒ 20.00–02.30 ⓝ Tram: 28, 12

BARS & CLUBS

Chapitô A creative space, a training school for performance arts, a theatre-cum-bar and a restaurant with a terrace. It's great for snacks but don't rely on the full menu always being on offer. ⓐ Rua Costa do Castelo 1–7 ⓣ (21) 885 5550 ⓦ www.chapito.org ⓒ 22.00–02.00 Wed–Mon, closed Tues

The Lux is a popular and trendy nightspot

Lux Bar Cool, stylish and impressive with large chairs and beds to slouch on and a birdcage to dance in, as well as a roof terrace. Located in a converted warehouse near Santa Apolónia Station, its main bar, club and video bar have different DJs every Thursday, Friday and Saturday. Av. Infante Dom Henrique, Armazém A (21) 882 0890 www.luxfragil.com 22.00–06.30 Tues–Sat, closed Sun & Mon Metro: Santa Apolonia

Onda Jazz This cavernous jazz bar hosts stellar jazz performers and freestyle jam sessions. Arco de Jesus 7 (21) 887 3064 www.ondajazz.com 20.00–02.00 Tues–Thur, 20.00–03.00 Fri & Sat, closed Sun & Mon Metro: Baixa Chiado

North of the Centre

This chapter covers the area from Praça dos Restauradores just north of the Baixa up to the Estádio da Luz football ground and the Colombo shopping centre, as well as from the Praça Duquade Saldanha west to the Parque Florestal de Monsanto. The tree-lined Avenida da Liberdade is one of the central arteries of the city and the Praça Marquês de Pombal is considered the 'very centre' of the city because other main roads radiate out from it. From Pombal to Amoreiras and north of Parque Eduardo VII (see page 87), the main focus is the business district, but there are also plenty of attractions, museums, palaces and gardens.

SIGHTS & ATTRACTIONS

Avenida da Liberdade

This attractive avenue, built in the style of a French boulevard, offers a pleasant walk from the Praça dos Restauradores to the Praça Marquês de Pombal. It is lined with elegant buildings such as the 1920s Tivoli cinema, the remodelled 1930s **Tivoli Lisboa Hotel** (ⓐ Av. da Liberdade 185 ⓣ (21) 319 8900 ⓦ www.tivolihotels.com) and the 19th-century **Cinemateca Portuguesa** just behind the hotel (ⓐ Rua Barata Salgueiro 39 ⓣ (21) 359 6200 ⓦ www.cinemateca.pt). Designer shops are dotted along its length, along with restaurants and cafés in the shade. Ⓜ Metro: Rossio/Restauradores/Marquês de Pombal; Bus: 12, 36, 44, 91, 709, 711, 732

Estádio da Luz (Stadium of Light)

This is the largest stadium in the country and the home ground for Sport Lisboa e Benfica (see page 32). The stadium also has facilities

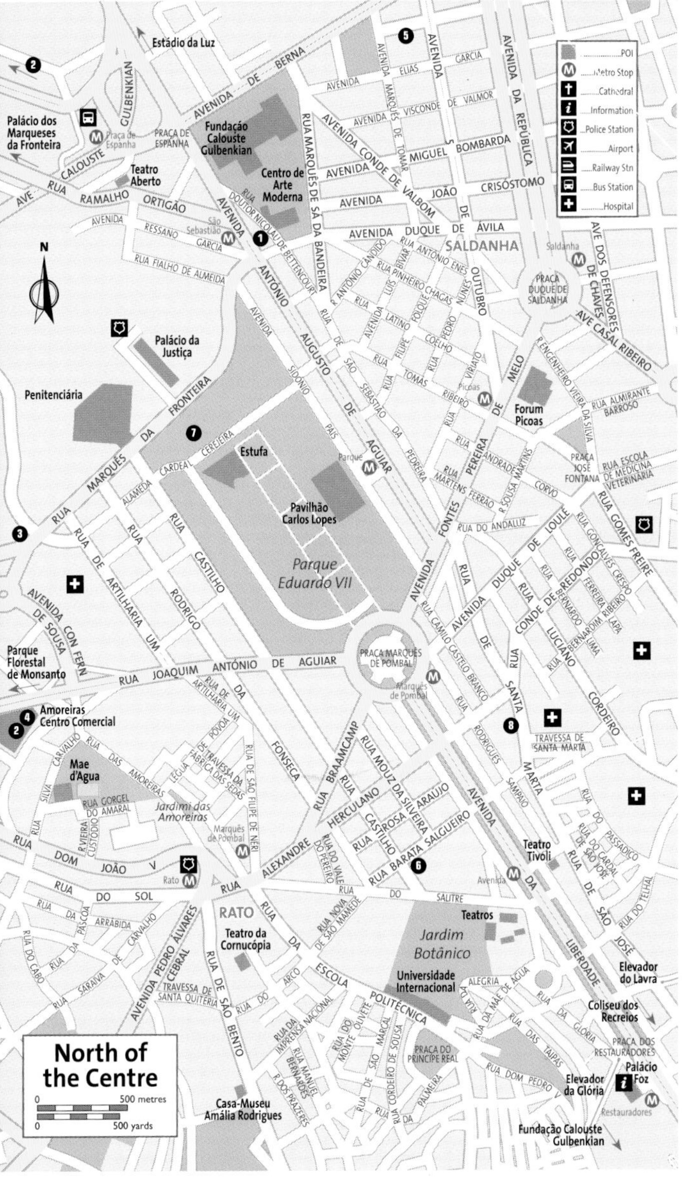
North of the Centre
0 500 metres
0 500 yards
POI
Metro Stop
Cathedral
Information
Police Station
Airport
Railway Stn
Bus Station
Hospital
N
Estádio da Luz
Palácio dos Marqueses da Fronteira
Praça de Espanha
PRAÇA DE ESPANHA
Fundação Calouste Gulbenkian
Centro de Arte Moderna
Teatro Aberto
São Sebastião
SALDANHA
Saldanha
PRAÇA DUQUE DE SALDANHA
Palácio da Justiça
Penitenciária
Picoas
Forum Picoas
Estufa
Parque
Pavilhão Carlos Lopes
Parque Eduardo VII
PRAÇA JOSÉ FONTANA
PRAÇA MARQUÊS DE POMBAL
Marquês de Pombal
Parque Florestal de Monsanto
Amoreiras Centro Comercial
Mae d'Agua
Jardim das Amoreiras
TRAVESSA DE SANTA MARTA
Teatro Tivoli
Avenida
Rato
RATO
Teatro da Cornucópia
Teatros
Jardim Botânico
Universidade Internacional
Elevador do Lavra
Coliseu dos Recreios
PRAÇA DOS RESTAURADORES
Palácio Foz
Elevador da Glória
Restauradores
PRAÇA DO PRINCIPE REAL
Casa-Museu Amália Rodrigues
Fundação Calouste Gulbenkian
AVENIDA DE BERNA
AVENIDA CALOUSTE GULBENKIAN
RUA RAMALHO ORTIGÃO
AVENIDA RESSANO GARCIA
RUA FIALHO DE ALMEIDA
RUA DOUTOR NICOLAU DE BETTENCOURT
AVENIDA ANTÓNIO AUGUSTO DE AGUIAR
RUA MARQUÊS DE SÁ DA BANDEIRA
AVENIDA CONDE DE VALBOM
AVENIDA MARQUÊS DE TOMAR
AVENIDA ELIAS GARCIA
AVENIDA VISCONDE DE VALMOR
AVENIDA MIGUEL BOMBARDA
AVENIDA JOÃO CRISÓSTOMO
AVENIDA DUQUE DE ÁVILA
AVENIDA DA REPÚBLICA
AVENIDA 5 DE OUTUBRO
AVE DOS DEFENSORES DE CHAVES
AVE CASAL RIBEIRO
RUA ANTÓNIO ENES
RUA PINHEIRO CHAGAS
RUA LATINO COELHO
RUA TOMÁS RIBEIRO
RUA VIRIATO
AVENIDA FONTES PEREIRA DE MELO
R ENGENHEIRO VIEIRA DA SILVA
RUA ALMIRANTE BARROSO
RUA ESCOLA DE MEDICINA VETERINÁRIA
RUA GOMES FREIRE
RUA MARTENS FERRÃO
RUA ANDRADE CORVO
RUA DO ANDALUZ
AVENIDA DUQUE DE LOULÉ
RUA CONDE DE REDONDO
RUA LUCIANO CORDEIRO
RUA CAMILO CASTELO BRANCO
RUA DE SANTA MARTA
RUA SÃO SEBASTIÃO DA PEDREIRA
AVENIDA SIDÓNIO PAIS
RUA CEREJEIRA
RUA MARQUÊS DA FRONTEIRA
ALAMEDA CARDEAL
RUA CASTILHO
RUA RODRIGO DA FONSECA
RUA DE ARTILHARIA UM
AVENIDA CON FERN DE SOUSA
RUA JOAQUIM ANTÓNIO DE AGUIAR
RUA DAS AMOREIRAS
RUA BRAAMCAMP
RUA MOUZ DA SILVEIRA
RUA ROSA ARAÚJO
RUA BARATA SALGUEIRO
RUA ALEXANDRE HERCULANO
AVENIDA DA LIBERDADE
RUA DO SALITRE
RUA DE SÃO JOSÉ
RUA DO PASSADIÇO
RUA DOM JOÃO V
RUA DO SOL
RUA DA ESCOLA POLITÉCNICA
RUA DE SÃO BENTO
AVENIDA PEDRO ÁLVARES CEBRAL
TRAVESSA DE SANTA QUITÉRIA
RUA DO ARCO
RUA DA IMPRENSA NACIONAL
RUA DO MONTE OLIVETE
RUA DE SÃO MARÇAL
RUA CORDEIRO DE SOUSA
RUA DOM PEDRO V
RUA DAS TAIPAS
RUA DA GLÓRIA
RUA DA MÃE DE ÁGUA
RUA NOVA DE SÃO MAMEDE
RUA DA ALEGRIA

for basketball, roller hockey, volleyball, five-a-side football, billiards and badminton. ⓐ Av. General Norton de Matos ⓣ (21) 721 9567 ⓦ www.slbenfica.pt Ⓝ Metro: Colegio Militar/Alto dos Moinhos; Bus: 3, 64, 729, 750, 765

Jardim das Amoreiras & Mãe d'Água (Amoreiras Gardens)
Inaugurated by the Marquês de Pombal in 1759, the Jardim das Amoreiras was filled with *amoreiras* – mulberry trees that were intended to boost the silk industry nearby. Today there are still some mulberry trees here, along with nine other species. At the back of the garden is the Mãe d'Água, a 19th-century reservoir decorated with *azulejos*. ⓐ Rua das Amoreiras Ⓝ Metro: Rato; Bus: 12, 48, 74, 701, 711

Jardim Botânico (Botanical Gardens)
Located in the grounds of Lisbon University's Faculty of Sciences, these gardens have the largest number of tall palms (*cicas*) in the country, along with numerous rare tropical flora, from palms to cacti, and fleshy plants. ⓐ Rua da Escola Politécnica 58 ⓣ (21) 392 1800 ⓦ www.jb.ul.pt Ⓛ 09.00–20.00 Mon–Fri, 10.00–20.00 Sat & Sun, Apr–Oct; 09.00–18.00 Mon–Fri, 10.00–18.00 Sat & Sun, Nov–Mar Ⓝ Metro: Rato; Bus: 711, 790. Admission charge

Palácio dos Marquêses da Fronteira (Fronteira Palace)
On a tour of this 17th-century palace you can see Mannerist architecture, baroque decoration and some fine examples of 17th- and 18th-century tiles. The formal gardens are geometric in style and filled with fountains and ponds, statues and still more tiles, this time illustrated with mythological scenes. ⓐ Largo São Domingos de Benfica 1 ⓣ (21) 778 2023 Ⓛ Guided tours 10.30–12.00 June–Sept; 11.00–12.00 Oct–May Ⓝ Metro: Alto dos Moinhos; Bus: 54, 64, 729, 746

An avenue of tranquillity at Jardim Botânico

Parque Eduardo VII

Named after the British king Edward VII, who visited Lisbon in 1903, this park lies on a slope at the top end of the Avenida da Liberdade. A network of pathways runs between green lawns, and you can visit the Estufa Fria and Estufa Quente, greenhouses with an array of exotic and rare plants. 09.00–19.30 Apr–Sept; 09.00–16.30 Oct–Mar
Metro: Marquês de Pombal; Bus: 12, 22, 36, 53, 83, 91, 702, 711

Parque Florestal de Monsanto

This park is Lisbon's biggest green space and it is better to explore it by car, as it is not really appropriate to walk around, both for safety and size. Within the vast expanse of the park, there is a campsite, mini-golf, tennis courts, swimming pool, an amphitheatre, shops and restaurant, as well as an exhibition centre and activities for children. Ⓐ Estra Barcal, Monte das Perdizes Bus: 714, 750

Praça Marquês de Pombal

Named after the man who rebuilt the Baixa following the 1755 earthquake, this double roundabout is the very centre of the city. From here main roads radiate out to different parts of the city, including south to the old quarters and the river, west to the business district and on to Sintra, and northeast towards the airport. Metro: Marquês de Pombal; Bus: 12, 22, 36, 44, 53, 83, 702, 711

Praça do Príncipe Real

In this large, romantic square you can relax on the benches in the shade or have a drink in the café. There is also a children's play area and an underground museum, the **Reservatório da Patriarcal** (10.00–18.00 Mon–Sat, closed Sun). It is set in an antique water cistern, part of the Mãe d'Água (see page 86). Metro: Rossio; Bus: 36, 92, 758, 773, 790

Praça dos Restauradores

Just north of Rossio Square at the bottom end of the Avenida da Liberdade, this large open square is dedicated to those who fought in the War of Restoration. On the left-hand side of the square is a former palace, Palácio Foz, which now houses the Ministry of Culture as well as the tourist office and shop. Metro: Restauradores; Bus: 36, 44, 91, 709, 711, 732, 745, 759

CULTURE

Coliseu dos Recreios

The Coliseum was originally built in 1890 but renovated in 1994 when Lisbon was European City of Culture. You can see both classical and popular music concerts here. ⓐ Rua das Portas de Santo Antão 96 ⓣ (21) 324 0585 ⓦ www.coliseulisboa.com ⓛ Box Office 13.00–19.30 Mon–Sat (closes half an hour before start time), closed Sun ⓡ Metro: Restauradores; Bus: 1, 2, 9, 11, 31, 32, 36, 39, 44, 45, 46, 59, 90, 92

Fundação Calouste Gulbenkian (Calouste Gulbenkian Foundation)

Portugal's most important cultural institution was conceived by Calouste Sarkis Gulbenkian in 1953. It comprises the country's most prestigious orchestra and choir, as well as museums, exhibition spaces, auditorium, arts library and lush gardens.

The Orchestra Gulbenkian has an annual season of concerts at home as well as touring internationally. The Coro Gulbenkian is a choir of more than 100 voices. It performs in a range of styles, from *a cappella* using a few choir members to large-scale performances, in conjunction with the Orchestra Gulbenkian.

CALOUSTE GULBENKIAN

Calouste Sarkis Gulbenkian (1869–1955) was the son of a merchant family of Armenian origins, who made his own fortune through investments in a Turkish petroleum company. During his life-long passion for the arts he built up an impressive collection, which can now be seen in the Museu Calouste Gulbenkian.

The **Museu Calouste Gulbenkian** (ⓦ www.museu.gulbenkian.pt) includes pieces collected by its founder throughout his lifetime. This is a real treasure trove, so you could spend quite some time here. It is organised geographically and chronologically, so you can explore the global treasures in two different circuits.

The **Centro de Arte Moderna José de Azeredo Perdigão (CAMJAP)**, Gulbenkian's modern art museum (ⓦ www.camjap.gulbenkian.pt), was founded in 1983 but its collection comprises work acquired by the Foundation since the 1950s. The most representative Portuguese artists from the 20th century are included, as well as some international modernist pieces. Highlights include works by Sonia and Robert Delaunay, Arpad, Pablo Gargallo, Henry Moore, Gilbert & George, and Antony Gormley. ⓐ Foundation and Museum: Av. de Berna 45A; CAMJAP: Rua Dr Nicolau de Bettencourt ⓣ Tickets (21) 782 3700; Museum (21) 782 3461; CAMJAP (21) 782 3474 ⓦ www.gulbenkian.pt; on-line tickets ⓦ www.bilheteira.gulbenkian.pt 10.00–18.00 Tues–Sun, closed Mon Metro: São Sebastião/Praça de Espanha; Bus: 16, 56, 718, 726, 742, 746. Admission charge

Teatro Aberto

Founded in 1982 by a group of theatre professionals, Teatro Aberto puts on fringe performances by its resident Novo Grupo de Teatro as well as companies from around the country and overseas. ⓐ Praça de Espanha ⓣ (21) 388 0089 ⓦ www.teatroaberto.com Metro: São Sebastião/Praça de Espanha; Bus: 16, 56, 726, 746

Teatro Tivoli

Designed by Paul Rino, the Tivoli was a cinema from when it opened in 1924 until 1988. Today it still has a screen but is primarily used for theatrical productions. ⓐ Av. da Liberdade 182–188 ⓣ (21) 357 2025

Sitting proudly outside the Museu Calouste Gulbenkian

www.teatro-tivoli.com Metro: Avenida; Bus: 36, 44, 45, 90, 91, 205, 207, 711, 732, 746

RETAIL THERAPY

Avenida da Liberdade has plenty of designer boutiques. Amoreiras (see page 22) is one of the older shopping centres but handy if you are staying in the business district; it has around 250 quality shops, a ten-screen cinema, supermarket, restaurants and parking. For a full-on shopping

day, take the metro to Colégio Militar for the Colombo shopping centre which has 400 wide-ranging stores with smart boutiques and trendier shops. For something more traditional, **Campo de Ourique** (ⓐ Rua Saraiva de Carvalho) has most of the international stores found in the shopping centres as well as local leather products and jewellery. There is a branch of the Spanish department store **El Corte Inglés** (ⓦ www.elcorteingles.pt) at Alto del Parque Eduardo VII, where you can find everything from clothes to stationery, as well as a supermarket.

TAKING A BREAK

You won't have to walk far to find a café along the Avenida da Liberdade or in Parque Eduardo VII. Many cafés have gardens and a play area for children nearby.

Cafetaria do CAMJAP (Gulbenkian) £ ❶ Great snacks, great surroundings: every box ticked, and reasonable prices. ⓐ Rua Dr Nicolau de Bettencourt ⓣ (21) 782 3474 ⓦ www.camjap.gulbenkian.pt ⓑ 10.00–17.45 Tues–Sun, closed Mon ⓝ Metro: Avenida

Shopping Centres £–££ ❷ All venues are a good option for lunch or coffee and a pastry: Colombo: ⓐ Av. Lusiada ⓦ www.colombo.pt ⓑ 10.00–00.00 ⓝ Metro: Colégio Militar; Amoreiras: ⓐ Rua Carlos Alberto da Mota Pinto, off Rua Joaquim Antonio de Aguiar ⓦ www.amoreiras.com ⓑ 10.00–00.00 ⓝ Metro: Avenida

AFTER DARK

There are some quality restaurants to be found along Avenida da Liberdade as well as around Parque Eduardo VII and Rato. There are

also some decent eateries in the Amoreiras shopping centre – it is not limited to fast food.

RESTAURANTS

A Valenciana £ ❸ Renowned for its charcoal-grilled meat and chicken, there is also fish on the menu. It is quite cheap, which

Not just shops, but architecture and statues on Avenida da Liberdade

makes this a good spot for lunch on a shoestring. ⓐ Rua Marquês da Fronteira 157 ⓣ (21) 388 4926 ⓦ www.avalenciana.restaunet.pt ⓛ 11.00–23.30 ⓜ Metro: Avenida

O Madeirense ££ ❹ This restaurant is popular for business lunches. Try some typical dishes from Madeira, including a *caldeira* (fish soup), tuna, swordfish and *espetada* (skewers of meat or fish). ⓐ Amoreiras Shopping Centre, Av. Engenheiro Duarte Pacheco, off Rua Joaquim Antonio de Aguiar ⓣ (21) 383 0827 ⓦ www.omadeirense.pt ⓛ 12.00–16.00, 19.00–23.00 Mon–Sat, closed Sun ⓜ Metro: Amoreiras

Paladar Zen ££ ❺ One of Lisbon's best vegetarian options, this stylish eatery serves tasty food that ranges in flavour from Mediterranean to Asian. ⓐ Av. Barbosa du Bocage 107C, off Av. da Republica ⓣ (21) 795 0009 ⓦ www.paladarzen.pt ⓛ 12.00–15.30, 19.30–23.00 Mon–Sat, closed Sun ⓜ Metro: Avenida

Varanda da União ££ ❻ Panoramic city views over the rooftops to the river. The menu is mainly Portuguese with house specialities including stuffed codfish and veal with lobster. ⓐ Rua Castilho 14C, 7th floor ⓣ (21) 314 1045 ⓦ www.varandadauniao.restaunet.pt ⓛ 12.00–15.00, 19.30–23.30 Mon–Fri, 19.30–23.30 Sat, closed Sun ⓜ Metro: Avenida

Eleven £££ ❼ The only Michelin-starred restaurant in Lisbon, Eleven has a prime location in the business district by the Amália Rodrigues Gardens. Modern and minimalist, the food is as internationally renowned as its chef, Joachim Koerper, with an innovative menu influenced by Mediterranean flavours. ⓐ Rua Marquês da Fronteira, Jardim Amália Rodrigues ⓣ (21) 386 2211 www.restauranteleven.com 12.30–15.00, 19.30–23.00 Tues–Sat, closed Sun & Mon Metro: Avenida

Luca £££ ❽ At lunchtime, this fashionable restaurant draws a buttoned-down business crowd but, come evening, it becomes a bustling eatery where some of Lisbon's best Italian food can be sampled. Rua Santa Marta 35 (21) 315 0212 www.luca.pt 12.30–15.00, 20.00–23.00 Mon–Thur, 12.30–15.00, 20.00–00.00 Fri, 20.00–00.00 Sat, closed Sun Metro: Avenida

BARS & CLUBS

Cinco Lounge This swish cocktail lounge by Principe Real attracts a trendy clientele for its wide variety of 100 cocktails and a relaxed yet stylish ambience. Rua Ruben A Leitão 17A (21) 342 4033 www.cincolounge.com 21.00–02.00 Tues–Sat, closed Sun & Mon Metro: Terminal do Rossio

Hot Clube de Portugal This is a legendary basement venue, the oldest jazz club in Portugal, with live music most nights. Next door there's a music school, which runs master classes and workshops. Praça da Alegria 39 (21) 346 7369 www.hcp.pt 23.00–02.00 Tues–Sat, closed Sun & Mon Metro: Avenida

Trumps Spread over two floors, this is the biggest and most popular gay venue in the city. There's a café with music and newspapers, while downstairs is split into the bar (with Brazilian music) and the club (dance music). Rua da Imprensa Nacional 104B (21) 397 1059 www.trumps.pt 23.45–06.00 Fri & Sat, closed Sun–Thur Metro: Rato

Belém & West Lisbon

Located on the banks of the Tagus, it was from Belém that many explorers set sail for Africa and the Americas. Many of its attractions are associated with or dedicated to them, including the Mosteiro dos Jerónimos (see page 98) and the Torre de Belém (see page 101). Belém has enough museums to keep you busy for several days, but the pick of the bunch is the Centro Cultural de Belém (see page 102), with its modern art and design museums.

Walk east along the river and you will come to the 25 de Abril Bridge, with the statue of Cristo Rei towering above it on the far side of the river. From the bridge onwards you come to the transformed Docas, the former docks that have now become one of the trendiest places to eat, drink and dance in the city. Just west of the docks is one of Portugal's most important museums, the Museu Nacional de Arte Antiga (see page 103), and north is Estrela where you can see the domes of the Basílica da Estrela (see below) and the Palácio de São Bento (see page 101), where parliament now sits.

SIGHTS & ATTRACTIONS

Basílica da Estrela

This church was built on the orders of Dona Maria I in the late 18th century. The Basilica can be easily spotted from various viewing points around the city, due to its large white dome and neoclassical façade. Inside it is decorated with Portuguese marble and has paintings by Italian masters. ⓐ Praça da Estrela ⓣ (21) 396 0915 ⓑ 07.45–20.00 ⓝ Tram: 28, 25; Bus: 709, 713, 720, 738

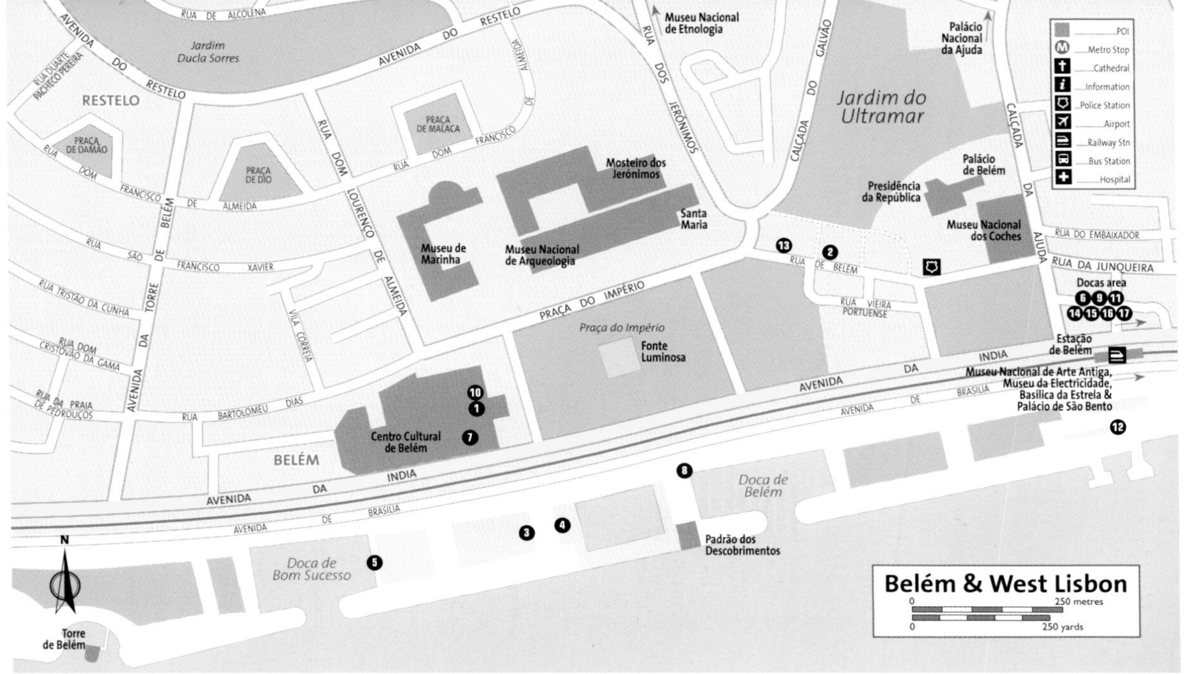

Belém & West Lisbon
0
250 metres
0
250 yards
POI
Metro Stop
Cathedral
Information
Police Station
Airport
Railway Stn
Bus Station
Hospital
RESTELO
BELÉM
Jardim Ducla Sorres
Jardim do Ultramar
Praça do Império
Doca de Belém
Doca de Bom Sucesso
Museu Nacional de Etnologia
Palácio Nacional da Ajuda
Palácio de Belém
Presidência da República
Museu Nacional dos Coches
Mosteiro dos Jerónimos
Santa Maria
Museu de Marinha
Museu Nacional de Arqueologia
Fonte Luminosa
Centro Cultural de Belém
Padrão dos Descobrimentos
Torre de Belém
Estação de Belém
Docas area
Museu Nacional de Arte Antiga, Museu da Electricidade, Basilica da Estrela & Palácio de São Bento
Praça de Malaca
Praça de Dio
Praça de Damão
Avenida do Restelo
Rua de Alcolena
Rua Duarte Pacheco Pereira
Rua Dom Francisco de Almeida
Rua Dom Lourenço de Almeida
Rua São Francisco Xavier
Rua Tristão da Cunha
Rua Dom Cristovão da Gama
Rua da Praia de Pedrouços
Avenida da Torre de Belém
Rua Bartolomeu Dias
Vila Correia
Praça do Império
Rua dos Jerónimos
Calçada do Galvão
Calçada da Ajuda
Rua de Belém
Rua Vieira Portuense
Rua do Embaixador
Rua da Junqueira
Avenida da India
Avenida de Brasília
N

GOLDEN AGE OF DISCOVERY

Portugal's seafaring success really began with Henry the Navigator, who led an expedition to North Africa in 1415. He was a leader in navigation and set up a school in the Algarve. Over the course of the next century, expeditions were sent to Africa, trade links were set up and islands were colonised – including the Canary Islands (later transferred to Castile), Madeira, the Azores, the Cape Verde Islands and São Tomé. Bartolomeu Dias eventually made it around the Cape of Good Hope in 1487, and Vasco da Gama opened up the spice trade route to India in 1498. João Cabral landed in Brazil in 1502 and trade posts were set up in Mozambique, Angola, Mombasa, Timor, China and Japan. The last leading maritime figure was Magellan, who circumnavigated the globe in 1522.

Mosteiro dos Jerónimos

At the heart of Belém, this former monastery was built on the grounds of a former church dedicated to the Virgin of Belém. It was later called the Mosteiro dos Jerónimos after the monks that lived there. Work began in 1501 on the orders of Dom Manuel I and took almost a century to complete. Highlights include the portals, which are adorned with statues and scenes from the life of São Jerónimo, the Church of Santa María with its cross shape, Manueline sculpting and tombs of Vasco da Gama and Luís de Camões and the cloisters. ⓐ Praça do Império ⓣ (21) 362 0034 ⓦ www.mosteirojeronimos.pt ⓛ 10.00–17.00 Tues–Sun, closed Mon, Oct–Apr; 10.00–18.30 Tues–Sun, closed Mon, May–Sept ⓝ Tram: 15; Bus: 28, 714, 729, 751. Admission charge

The Mosteiro dos Jerónimos, viewed from Padrão dos Descobrimentos

Padrão dos Descobrimentos (Discoveries Monument)

This impressive building is 50 m (164 ft) high and dedicated to Portugal's Golden Age of Discovery. Built by architect José Cotinelli Telmo and sculptor Leopoldo de Almeida, it was inaugurated in 1960 to mark the 500th anniversary of the death of Henry the Navigator. Along the side of the building is a sculpture depicting a Portuguese *caravela* (boat) with the most renowned of the country's seafarers looking out to sea. Henry the Navigator is at the prow, with Vasco da Gama, Pedro Alvares Cabral and Ferdinand Magellan among the other figures. Inside there are exhibition rooms and you can take the lift to the top of the monument for panoramic views of the Tagus and the city. Av. de Brasília (21) 303 1950 10.00–19.00 Tues–Sun, closed Mon, May–Sept; 10.00–18.00 Tues–Sun, closed Mon, Oct–Apr Tram: 15; Bus: 28, 714, 727, 729, 751. Admission charge

A fitting tribute to Portugal's great explorers, Padrão dos Descobrimentos

Palácio de Belém

Located behind the Museu Nacional dos Coches, this 16th-century pink palace can be seen from the main road. Today it is the official residence of the President of Portugal and can only be visited by prior arrangement. Calçada da Ajuda 11 (21) 361 4600 By appointment only Tram: 15

Palácio Nacional da Ajuda

Take a detour towards the Parque Florestal de Monsanto to see this neoclassical palace, built for the royal family who occupied it from 1861 until 1910. It became a museum in 1938 and holds an important collection of decorative arts from the 15th to the 20th centuries, including pieces in gold, jewellery, paintings, sculpture, furniture, textiles and ceramics. Ⓐ Largo da Ajuda Ⓣ (21) 363 7095 Ⓛ 10.00–17.00 Thur–Tues, closed Wed Ⓝ Tram: 18; Bus: 60, 729, 742

Palácio de São Bento/Assambleia da República

This parliamentary building occupies a former convent. Once a month there are guided tours to see parts of the convent church and the refectory with its tiled panels, the grandiose official reception rooms, plus the coats of arms and statues. Tours must be booked in advance. Ⓐ Rua de São Bento Ⓣ (21) 391 9625 Ⓦ www.parlamento.pt/visita Ⓛ Tours 14.00 & 15.00 last Sat of the month Ⓝ Tram: 28; Bus: 706, 727, 773

Torre de Belém

This riverside tower was built from 1514–20 as part of a defence system for the River Tagus and as homage to Lisbon's patron saint, São Vicente da Fora. It is also a symbol of Portugal's maritime exploits and in 1983 was declared a UNESCO World Heritage Site. You can see some of the best examples of Manueline architecture here, particularly the stone ropes that encircle the building, as well as the heraldic emblems, the cross of the Order of Christ and the famous carving of a rhinoceros. If you climb the steps to the top of the tower you will find fabulous city and river views. Ⓐ Av. de Brasilia Ⓣ (21) 362 0034 Ⓛ 10.00–17.00 Tues–Sun, closed Mon, Oct–Apr; 10.00–18.30 Tues–Sun, closed Mon, May–Sept Ⓝ Tram: 15; Bus: 729. Admission charge

CULTURE

Casa-Museu Amália Rodrigues (see map on page 85)

This small museum pays tribute to the internationally famous *fado* diva Amália Rodrigues, who lived in this house until her death in 1999. The now renovated interiors display the original decorations and furnishings as well as Amália's personal objects such as dresses, jewellery and shoes. ⓐ Rua de São Bento 193 ⓣ (21) 397 1896 ⓛ 10.00–13.00, 14.00–18.00 Tues–Sun, closed Mon ⓝ Metro: Rato; Bus: 6, 58, 100

Centro Cultural de Belém

This modern cultural centre was completed in 1988 and comprises an exhibition centre, performance centre and meeting centre. The meeting centre is a high-tech facility that caters for meetings and conferences and includes shops, a restaurant (see page 105), two bars and the CCB's administration centre.

The performance centre hosts some of the best performances of opera, ballet, classical music, jazz and theatre in the city. The exhibition centre comprises four galleries with temporary exhibitions by both Portuguese and internationally renowned modern and contemporary artists. The Museu do Design is also housed here, where you can see exhibitions of architecture, design and photography. ⓐ Praça do Império ⓣ (21) 361 2400 ⓦ www.ccb.pt ⓛ 08.00–20.00 Mon–Fri, 10.00–19.00 Sat & Sun (until 02.00 when there are performances) ⓝ Tram: 15; Bus: 28, 714, 727, 729, 751

Museu da Electricidade (Electricity Museum)

The former Tejo Power Station houses a museum where you can admire the industrial beauty of this architectural landmark and learn about various electrical phenomena. ⓐ Av. de Brasília ⓣ (21) 002 8190 ⓦ www.fundacao.edp.pt ⓛ 10.00–18.30 Tues–Sun, closed Mon ⓝ Tram: 15; Bus: 28, 714, 727, 729, 751. Admission charge

Museu de Marinha (Naval Museum)

This museum occupies what were once the north and west wings of the Mosteiro dos Jerónimos. It includes models of boats from the

MANUELINO

While the Reconquest had led to the building of Gothic churches such as the Sé (see page 78), from 1480–1540 a new architectural style emerged. *Manuelino*, or Manueline architecture, named after Dom Manuel I, the king during this period, explored elaborate decoration reflecting themes of maritime voyages, heraldry and religion. Dom Manuel I commissioned numerous buildings, including the Mosteiro dos Jerónimos and Torre de Belém (see pages 98 & 101).

Golden Age of Discovery as well as royal, merchant, fishing and leisure boats. Ⓐ Praça do Império Ⓣ (21) 362 0019 Ⓦ www.museu.marinha.pt Ⓛ 10.00–18.00 Tues–Sun, closed Mon, Apr–Sept (until 17.00 Oct–Mar) Ⓝ Tram: 15; Bus: 28, 714, 727, 729, 751. Admission charge

Museu Nacional de Arqueologia (National Archaeological Museum)

This museum has occupied the former monks' quarters at the Mosteiro since 1893. Here you can see displays of archaeology, ethnography, coins, jewellery, stone engravings, sculpture, mosaics and physical anthropology. Ⓐ Praça do Império Ⓣ (21) 362 0000 Ⓦ www.mnarqueologia-ipmuseus.pt Ⓛ 10.00–18.00 Tues–Sun, closed Mon Ⓝ Tram: 15; Bus: 28. Admission charge

Museu Nacional de Arte Antiga (National Museum of Ancient Art)

This museum in Santos is also known as the Museu das Janelas Verdes (the Green Shutter Museum) because of the shutters on the former 17th-century palace in which it is housed. Highlights include the collection of Portuguese and European paintings from the

15th to the 19th centuries, and religious sculpture from the 18th century. Also look out for the pieces collected during Portugal's seafaring travels to Africa, India, China and Japan, dating from the 16th to the 18th centuries. ⓐ Rua das Janelas Verdes ⓣ (21) 391 2800 ⓦ www.mnarteantiga-ipmuseus.pt ◷ 10.00–18.00 Wed–Sun, 14.00–18.00 Tues, closed Mon Ⓝ Tram: 15; Bus: 28, 706, 714, 727. Admission charge

Museu Nacional dos Coches (National Coach Museum)
Housed in a former royal riding school, this museum has a collection of coaches from the 16th to the 19th centuries, as well as a collection of oil paintings of the Portuguese royal family. ⓐ Rua Afonso de Albuquerque ⓣ (21) 361 0850 ⓦ www.museudoscoches-ipmuseus.pt ◷ 10.00–18.00 Tues–Sun, closed Mon Ⓝ Tram: 15; Bus: 28, 714, 727, 729, 751. Admission charge

Museu Nacional de Etnologia (National Ethnology Museum)
With a 30,000-strong collection of artefacts, this museum showcases a display on rural life in Portugal as well as items from the former Portuguese colonies, from sculpture to fabrics and paintings. ⓐ Av. Ilha da Madeira ⓣ (21) 304 1160 ⓦ www.mnetnologia-ipmuseus.pt ◷ 14.00–18.00 Tues, 10.00–18.00 Wed–Sun, closed Mon Ⓝ Bus: 28, 714, 732. Admission charge

TAKING A BREAK

This area offers a wide choice of places to stop for lunch. If you fancy a walk along the river, just east past the 25 de Abril Bridge is the renovated Docas with a large number of cafés, open-air terraces and restaurants.

Cafeteria Quadrante £ ❶ Inside the Centro Cultural de Belém, it overlooks the river. ⓐ Praça do Império ⓣ (21) 362 2888 ⓦ www.ccb.pt ◷ 10.00–22.00 Mon–Fri, 10.00–21.00 Sat & Sun ⓝ Tram: 15

Antiga Confeitaria de Belém ££ ❷ Belém's most famous café. Try their *pasteis de Belém* (custard tart). ⓐ Rua de Belém 84–92 ⓣ (21) 363 7423 ⓦ www.pasteisdebelem.pt ◷ 08.00–23.00 Mon–Sat, 08.00–22.00 Sun, Nov–Apr; 08.00–00.00 May–Oct ⓝ Tram: 15

Belem Bar Café ££ ❸ Stylish bar, café and restaurant with a terrace and great river views. ⓐ Av. de Brasília, Pavilhão Poente ⓣ (21) 362 4232 ⓦ www.belembarcafe.com ◷ 12.00–15.00, 20.00–02.00 Tues–Fri, 12.00–15.00, 20.00–05.00 Sat & Sun, closed Mon ⓝ Tram: 15

Café In ££ ❹ Typical Portuguese café serving coffee, tea, croissants, cakes, toasted sandwiches and light lunches. ⓐ Av. de Brasília 311

Crossing the Tagus; in the background, 25 de Abril Bridge and Cristo Rei *statue*

Take a tour bus around Belém

(21) 362 6248 www.gastronomias.com/cafe-in/ 10.00–03.00 Tram: 15

Vela Latina ££ 5 Serves both Portuguese and international food. Good for a light lunch. Doca do Bom Sucesso (21) 301 7118 www.velalatina.pt 12.30–15.00, 20.00–23.30 Mon–Sat, closed Sun Tram: 15

AFTER DARK

Belém's open aspect and riverside location make it a favourite hangout for eating and drinking while watching the sunset before heading out to a club. Back towards the old city are the renovated Docas by

the 25 de Abril Bridge. During the last decade the Docas have been transformed from grim dockland warehouses into one of the most vibrant and trendy areas in the city for restaurants, bars and clubs.

RESTAURANTS & BARS

Alentejo nas Docas £ ❻ Spread over three floors and with a terrace, it offers traditional dishes from the Alentejo region. ⓐ Doca de Santo Amaro ⓣ (21) 390 8024 ⓦ www.alentejodocas.com ⓛ 12.00–15.30, 19.30–23.30 ⓜ Metro: São Paulo

Bar do Terraço £ ❼ Almost every evening during the summer you can come and listen to live jazz and other concerts. Nice nibbles, too. ⓐ CCB, Praça do Império ⓣ (21) 361 2613 ⓦ www.ccb.pt ⓛ 12.30–20.00 Mon–Fri, 12.30–19.00 Sat & Sun

Já Sei £ ❽ This terraced riverside restaurant has plenty of seafood and fish on the menu, as well as peppered steak and roast lamb. ⓐ Av. de Brasília 202 ⓣ (21) 301 5969 ⓛ 12.30–15.30, 19.30–23.00 Mon–Fri, 12.30–15.30 Sat & Sun

Tertulia do Tejo £ ❾ Spread over two floors, this relaxed restaurant serves typical Portuguese dishes such as *caldo verde*. Its *pratos do día* (daily specials) are good value. ⓐ Doca de Santo Amaro ⓣ (21) 395 5552 ⓦ www.tertuliadotejo.com ⓛ 12.15–16.00, 19.45–23.30

A Commenda ££ ❿ Located inside the Centro Cultural de Belém, this sophisticated restaurant is renowned for its privileged position overlooking the river, as well as its quality. ⓐ CCB, Praça do Império ⓣ (21) 364 8561 ⓦ www.ccb.pt ⓛ 12.30–15.00, 19.30–22.30 Mon–Sat, 13.00–16.00 Sun

Blues Café ££ ⓫ A mixture of restaurant, bar and club, this popular venue serves Cajun food and has four bars. ⓐ Rua da Cintura do Porto, Edifício 226, Armazém H ⓣ (21) 395 7085 ⓦ www.bluescafe.pt ◔ 20.00–03.30 Tues–Thur, restaurant service until 01.00; 20.00–05.00 Fri & Sat, closed Sun & Mon

Piazza di Mare ££ ⓬ You'll find all the old favourites from pizza to pasta to Parma ham and mozzarella and tomato salad – and it won't break the bank. ⓐ Av. de Brasília, Pavilhão Poente ⓣ (21) 362 4235 ⓦ www.piazzadimare.com ◔ 12.30–16.00, 20.00–00.30

Rosa dos Mares ££ ⓭ The restaurant is named after a legend concerning sailors who are alleged to have seen roses floating in the sea. Today the restaurant even has a codfish dish named after the 'sea roses', as well as heavenly charcoal-grilled fish and the absolutely splendid *arroz de mariscos* (shellfish rice). ⓐ Rua de Belém 110 ⓣ (21) 362 1811 ⓦ www.rosadosmares.restaunet.pt ◔ 12.00–15.00, 19.00–22.00

Speakeasy ££ ⓮ Serving Portuguese and international food until the club starts, there's music most nights. ⓐ Cais das Oficinas, Rocha do Conde de Óbidos ⓣ (21) 396 4257 ⓦ www.speakeasy-bar.com ◔ 20.00–03.00 Mon–Thur, until 04.00 Fri & Sat, restaurant service until 23.00, closed Sun

Uai! ££ ⓯ Brazilian restaurant with a menu that includes fried *cassava* (manioc), spare ribs, black beans and stuffed pumpkin, as well as *caipirinhas* (a Brazilian cocktail made with *cachaça*, limes, sugar and ice). ⓐ Rocha do Conde de Óbidos, Cais de Oficinas ⓣ (21) 390 0111 ⓦ www.uai.restaunet.pt ◔ 13.00–15.00, 20.00–23.00 Tues–Sun, closed lunch Tues & Wed, closed dinner Sun, closed Mon

Alcântara Café £££ ⓰ A 1920s-style restaurant decorated in wood, leather and velvet, this place serves a mixture of Portuguese specialities and French cuisine. Fish features highly on the menu. ⓐ Rua Maria Luisa Holstein 15 ⓣ (21) 363 7176 ⓦ www.alcantaracafe.com ⓛ 20.00–03.00 restaurant service until 01.00 Mon–Sun

Kais £££ ⓱ This chic restaurant in a converted warehouse has a cool industrial design and delicious Portuguese fare. ⓐ Cais da Viscondessa, Rua da Cintura ⓣ (21) 393 2930 ⓦ www.kais-k.com ⓛ 20.00–01.00 Mon–Sat, closed Sun

BARS & CLUBS

Dock's Club Late-night club that's popular with the younger crowd. It has theme nights and 'ladies' nights'. ⓐ Rua da Cintura do Porto de Lisboa 226 ⓣ (21) 395 0856 ⓛ 23.00–06.00 Tues–Sat, closed Sun & Mon

Indochina Club with a Vietnamese-Oriental theme that's one of the trendiest on the Docas. Most popular for its club nights with a mix of pop and the latest dance tunes. ⓐ Rua da Cintura do Porto de Lisboa, Armazém H ⓣ (21) 395 5875 ⓛ 23.00–06.00 Tues–Sat, closed Sun & Mon

Kremlin A favourite for dance music, this club starts late and stays open until breakfast. ⓐ Rua das Escadinhas da Praia 5 (Av. 24 de Julio) ⓣ (21) 395 7101 ⓛ 00.00–08.00 Wed–Sat, closed Sun–Tues

Queens The décor of this club with an enormous dance floor is distinctly 1970s and it has three bars and views of the river. ⓐ Rua da Cintura do Porto de Lisboa, Armazém H ⓣ (21) 395 5870 ⓛ 23.00–06.00 Tues–Sat, closed Sun & Mon

Parque das Nações

The Parque das Nações was built for Expo '98 and is a showcase of modern architecture. Stretched along a 3-km (2-mile) length of the River Tagus in east Lisbon, it doesn't have a crumbling building in sight (though it does have a remarkably tall one, the former Vasco da Gama Tower, which is not open to the public). Just a ten-minute bus ride from the airport, and with a major train station, it is here that Portugal travels into the 21st century.

SIGHTS & ATTRACTIONS

The easiest way to get to Parque das Nações is the short metro ride to Oriente. You arrive by the shopping centre and once outside you will see the cable car along the riverfront with the Vasco da Gama Bridge at one end and the Oceanário at the other. In front are the Pavilhão Atlântico (see page 113) and the Doca dos Olivais.

Oceanário de Lisboa (Lisbon Oceanarium)

Located at the southern end of the Doca dos Olivais, the Oceanário is well worth the pricey ticket. Inside are four areas representing coastal habitats of the North Atlantic, Antarctic, Temperate Pacific and Tropical Indian oceans, connected by a central tank to create the illusion of a single ocean. The Global Ocean is 49 m (160 ft) high and is the centrepiece of the exhibition. You can come face to face with sharks, rays and barracuda, conga eels, giant grouper and tuna, puffins, penguins, seals, seahorses, sea urchins, anemones, corals and jellyfish, to mention just a few. ⓐ Explanada Dom Carlos I ⓣ (21) 891 7002 ⓦ www.oceanario.pt ⓛ 10.00–19.00 Apr–Oct (until 18.00 Nov–Mar) ⓝ Metro: Oriente; Bus: 5, 25, 28, 44, 708, 750, 759. Admission charge

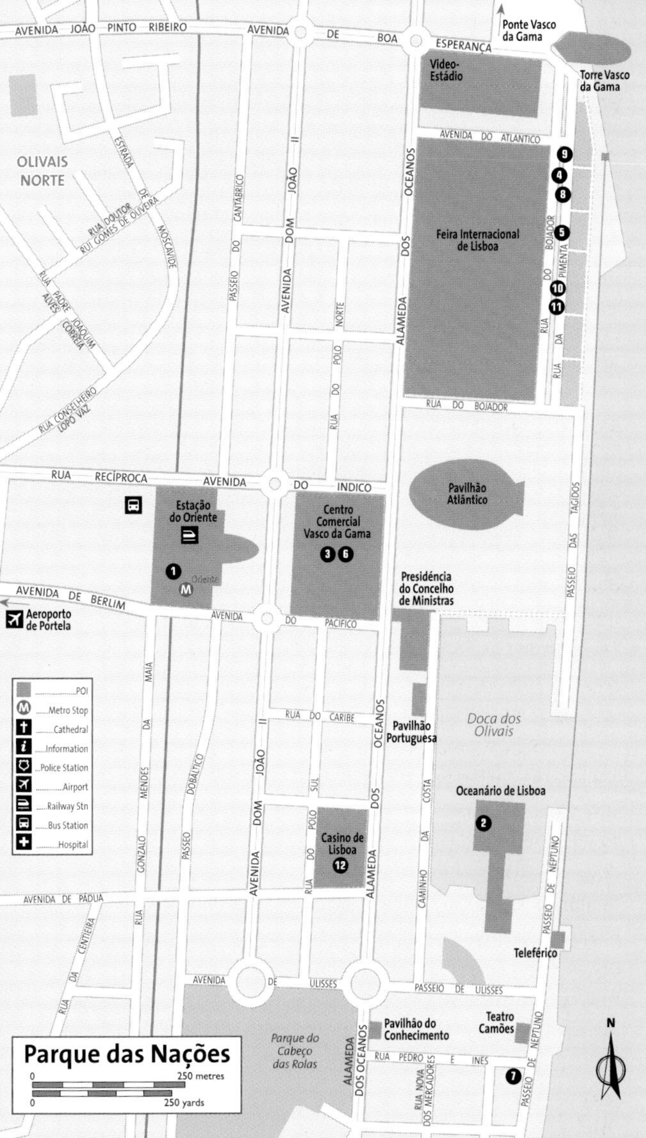

Parque das Nações
0
250 metres
0
250 yards
AVENIDA JOÃO PINTO RIBEIRO
AVENIDA DE BOA ESPERANÇA
Ponte Vasco da Gama
Torre Vasco da Gama
Video-Estádio
AVENIDA DO ATLANTICO
Feira Internacional de Lisboa
OLIVAIS NORTE
ESTRADA DE MOSCAVIDE
RUA DOUTOR RUI GOMES DE OLIVEIRA
RUA PADRE ALVES CORREIA
JOAQUIM
RUA CONSELHEIRO LOPO VAZ
PASSEIO DO CANTABRICO
AVENIDA DOM JOÃO II
ALAMEDA DOS OCEANOS
RUA DO POLO NORTE
RUA DA PIMENTA
RUA DO BOJADOR
RUA RECÍPROCA
AVENIDA DO INDICO
Estação do Oriente
Oriente
Centro Comercial Vasco da Gama
Pavilhão Atlântico
PASSEIO DAS TAGIDOS
Presidência do Concelho de Ministras
AVENIDA DE BERLIM
Aeroporto de Portela
AVENIDA DO PACIFICO
RUA DO CARIBE
Pavilhão Portuguesa
Doca dos Olivais
Oceanário de Lisboa
CAMINHO DA COSTA
RUA GONZALO MENDES DA MAIA
PASSEIO DOBALTICO
RUA DO POLO SUL
Casino de Lisboa
PASSEIO DE NEPTUNO
AVENIDA DE PÁDUA
RUA DA CENTIEIRA
Teleférico
AVENIDA DE ULISSES
PASSEIO DE ULISSES
Parque do Cabeço das Rolas
Pavilhão do Conhecimento
Teatro Camões
RUA PEDRO E INES
RUA NOVA DOS MERCADORES
N
1
2
3
4
5
6
7
8
9
10
11
12
POI
Metro Stop
Cathedral
Information
Police Station
Airport
Railway Stn
Bus Station
Hospital

The largest Oceanarium in Europe is in the Parque das Nações

Pavilhão do Conhecimento (Knowledge Pavilion)

This is an interactive science and technology museum that aims to make science available to all. Highlights include displays on mathematics, the 'Flying Bicycle' and nanotechnology. ⓐ Alameda dos Oceanos ⓣ (21) 891 7100 ⓦ www.pavconhecimento.pt ⓑ 10.00–18.00 Tues–Fri, 11.00–19.00 Sat–Sun, closed Mon ⓝ Metro: Oriente; Bus: 5, 25, 28, 44, 708, 750, 759. Admission charge

Teleférico (Cable Car)

If you get a thrill from heights and you don't want to walk the distance between the Oceanário and the Vasco da Gama Tower, then the cable car is a suitable option. You'll also get a bird's-eye view over the park as you pass the Pavilhão Atlântico concert venue,

PARQUE DAS NAÇÕES CARD

This card (€15.50) includes a visit to the Oceanário and Pavilhão do Conhecimento, a single or return trip on the cable car, unlimited rides on the tourist train that travels around the park, 20 per cent off bicycle hire at Tejo Bike (see page 148) and 15 per cent off at some restaurants. You can purchase the cards from the Oceanário or the Parque das Nações Information Desk.

the huge Exhibition Centre, restaurants and the former Vasco da Gama Tower. ⓐ Doca dos Olivais, Parque das Nações ⓣ (21) 895 6143 ⓛ 11.00–19.00 Mon–Fri, 10.00–19.00 Sat & Sun ⓝ Metro: Oriente; Bus: 5, 25, 28, 44, 708, 750, 759. Admission charge

CULTURE

Casino de Lisboa

Aside from the slot machines, roulette, blackjack and poker, there's also an auditorium with international and Portuguese music, dance and theatre productions, a lounge bar with live music, several bars linked to the gaming rooms, and three restaurants. ⓐ Alameda dos Oceanos ⓣ (21) 892 9000 ⓦ www.casino-lisboa.pt ⓛ 15.00–03.00 ⓝ Metro: Oriente; Bus: 5, 25, 28, 44, 708, 750, 759

Pavilhão Atlântico

One of the city's major concert and sports venues, this state-of-the-art pavilion is easy to find on the riverfront. ⓐ Rossio dos Olivais ⓣ (21) 891 8409 ⓦ www.pavilhaoatlantico.pt ⓝ Metro: Oriente; Bus: 5, 25, 28, 44, 708, 750, 759

Teatro Camões

Home of the National Ballet of Portugal, this theatre's calendar focuses on dance performances by other leading companies. ⓐ Passeio de Neptuno ⓣ (21) 892 3470 ⓦ www.cnb.pt Ⓝ Metro: Oriente; Bus: 5, 25, 28, 44, 708, 750, 759

RETAIL THERAPY

Centro Comercial Vasco da Gama (ⓐ Av. Dom João II ⓣ (21) 893 0600 ⓦ www.centrovascodagama.pt ◷ 09.00–00.00 Ⓝ Metro: Oriente) is the main shopping area. Spread over four floors, it includes fashion stores such as Zara, Mango, Cortefiel, Massimo Dutti, Lacoste and Bershka, as well as shoes, sports, gifts, music, furniture, jewellery and perfume shops. There is also a cinema and a huge supermarket.

There are a few outlets along the Alameda dos Oceanos and Rua da Ilha dos Amores, such as car hire, art galleries, stationery, furniture and toys. There is also a craft shop along Rua da Pimenta.

TAKING A BREAK

There are several places and boutique cafés for coffees and snacks, and plenty of bars if you fancy a gin and tonic with a river view.

Baskin-Robbins £ ❶ In Oriente Station, and just right for a snack and a cuppa. ⓐ Estação Oriente, Loja G103 ⓣ (21) 941 9575 ◷ 08.00–21.00 Ⓝ Metro: Oriente; Bus: 5, 28, 44

Il Caffè di Roma £ ❷ By the Oceanário, an Italian chain of boutique cafés that serve good coffee – you can have it with cream, ice cream or alcohol. ⓐ Edificio Oceanário de Lisboa, Esplanada Dom Carlos I

The Teleférico takes you from the Oceanário to the Vasco da Gama Bridge

www.ilcaffediroma.pt 10.00–20.00 Metro: Oriente; Bus: 5, 28, 44

Centro Comercial Vasco da Gama £ ❸ There is no shortage of places to stop for refreshment and a rest from tiring shopping (see opposite).

AFTER DARK

There is a wide range of restaurants and bars all along the riverfront between the Pavilhão Atlântico and the Vasco da Gama Tower.

100 Norte £ ❹ A restaurant by day and bar-club by night, there is a large terrace and indoor seating. The menu includes steaks, pizza, pasta, fish and sandwiches, as well as a children's menu. The bar-club has karaoke and ladies' nights. ⓐ Rua do Bojador 107 ⓣ (21) 895 8248 ◔ 12.00–05.00 Tues–Sun, closed Mon & Nov–Mar ⓜ Metro: Oriente

Café da Palha £ ❺ Caters for large groups and serves traditional Portuguese food. It is particularly good for steaks, grills and salads. They have karaoke and club nights until the early hours of the morning. ⓐ Rua da Pimenta 75–79 ⓣ (21) 895 5915 ◔ 16.00–05.00 Sun & Mon, Wed & Thur, 11.00–05.00 Fri & Sat, closed Tues ⓜ Metro: Oriente

Cervejeira Lusitana £ ❻ Portuguese beer and steak chain restaurant, with a kids' menu. ⓐ Centro Comercial Vasco da Gama, 3rd floor ⓣ (21) 895 8071 ⓦ www.lusitana.com ◔ 11.00–00.00

Mestre Doce £ ❼ Small family-style restaurant, serving home-cooked Portuguese cuisine such as prawn rice and steaks, as well as good desserts. ⓐ Passeio de Neptuno 3 ⓣ (21) 894 6043 ◔ 08.00–00.00 ⓜ Metro: Oriente

El Tapas ££ ❽ Typically Spanish restaurant serving tapas, paellas and other Iberian specialties. It is located by the former Torre

One of the stunning fountains in Parque das Nações

de Vasco da Gama. Rua da Pimenta 99–101 (21) 896 6900 12.00–01.00 Mon–Fri, 12.00–03.00 Sat & Sun Metro: Oriente

Havana ££ 9 Typically Cuban restaurant looking out on to the former Vasco da Gama Tower and Bridge. Specialities include steak Che Guevara, fried prawns and Caribbean salad. Rua da Pimenta 115–117 (21) 895 7116 12.00–04.00 Metro: Oriente

Passeio do Oriente ££ 10 With a large terrace and two floors inside, it serves traditional Portuguese lunches, dinners and snacks, German beers, sangria, *caipirinhas* and shots. There is also live music, karaoke and Spanish dancing. Rua da Pimenta 51

ⓣ (21) 895 6147 ⓦ www.passeioriente.com ⓛ 12.00–02.00 Sun–Tues & Thur, until 04.00 Fri & Sat, closed Wed ⓜ Metro: Oriente

Senhor Peixe ££ ⓫ Specialises in fish dishes, such as shrimps with garlic to start, shrimp soup, fish stew, lobster rice, grilled squid, grouper or langoustines. They also serve vegetable soup and steaks. ⓐ Rua da Pimenta 35–37 ⓣ (21) 895 5892 ⓦ www.cidiarte.pt/senhorpeixe ⓛ 12.00–15.30, 19.00–22.30 Thur–Sun, closed Mon–Wed ⓜ Metro: Oriente

Pragma £££ ⓬ Celebrity chef Fausto Airoldi serves his signature dishes at this elegant restaurant inside Casino Lisboa. The *degustation* menu is pricey but a gastronomic feast worth the splurge. ⓐ Alameda dos Oceanos ⓣ (21) 892 9043 ⓦ www.pragmalx.com ⓛ 19.30–00.00 Tues–Sun, closed Mon

BARS & CLUBS

Irish & Co More of a pub than a restaurant, it serves an innovative mixture of Irish and Portuguese food including fresh fish of the day and 'stout' steak, as well as pints of Guinness and Kilkenny. ⓐ Rua da Pimenta 57–61 ⓣ (21) 894 0558 ⓦ www.irishco.com.pt ⓛ 12.30–04.00 ⓜ Metro: Oriente

Peter Café Sport This bar is a replica of the famous bar in Faial, Azores, where sailors would stop to pick up their messages and have a gin and tonic. If you want something to eat, try the Steak Peter or a toasted sandwich. ⓐ Rua da Pimenta 39–41 ⓣ (21) 895 0060 ⓛ 12.00–02.00 ⓜ Metro: Oriente

---

Enjoy a walk in Cabo da Roca, Europe's most westerly point

OUT OF TOWN
trips

Cascais & Estoril

Just 24 km (15 miles) west of Lisbon, Estoril and Cascais provide the perfect beach and golf locations within easy reach of the capital's culture and attractions. The popularity of the Estoril coast began in 1889 with the opening of the train line from Lisbon. Today surfing and sailing are popular and there are several first-class golf courses (see page 33), a race track (see page 32), marina and a casino. Popular with kids and the young crowd because of the beach, surfing and clubs, Estoril also features plenty of cultural activities: picturesque museum-mansions, cultural centres, open-air entertainment and the famous Casino Estoril (Estoril Casino, see page 122) – as well as the relaxing atmosphere, good seafood and fresh sea air.

The Estoril Coast Tourism website covers the region west of Oeiras and south of Sintra, and includes Estoril and Cascais, as well as various coastal and inland towns and villages. Ⓦ www.estorilcoast-tourism.com

GETTING THERE

By rail

The Cascais train line runs from Cais do Sodré along the coast via Alcântara Mar and Belém. The journey from Cais do Sodré to Cascais takes 33–40 minutes, from Alcântara 24–31 minutes and from Belém 28–50 minutes, depending on whether you take a fast or slow train. Estoril is two stops before Cascais, so you can deduct about five minutes from the journey time. You can check the exact schedule at Ⓦ www.cp.pt

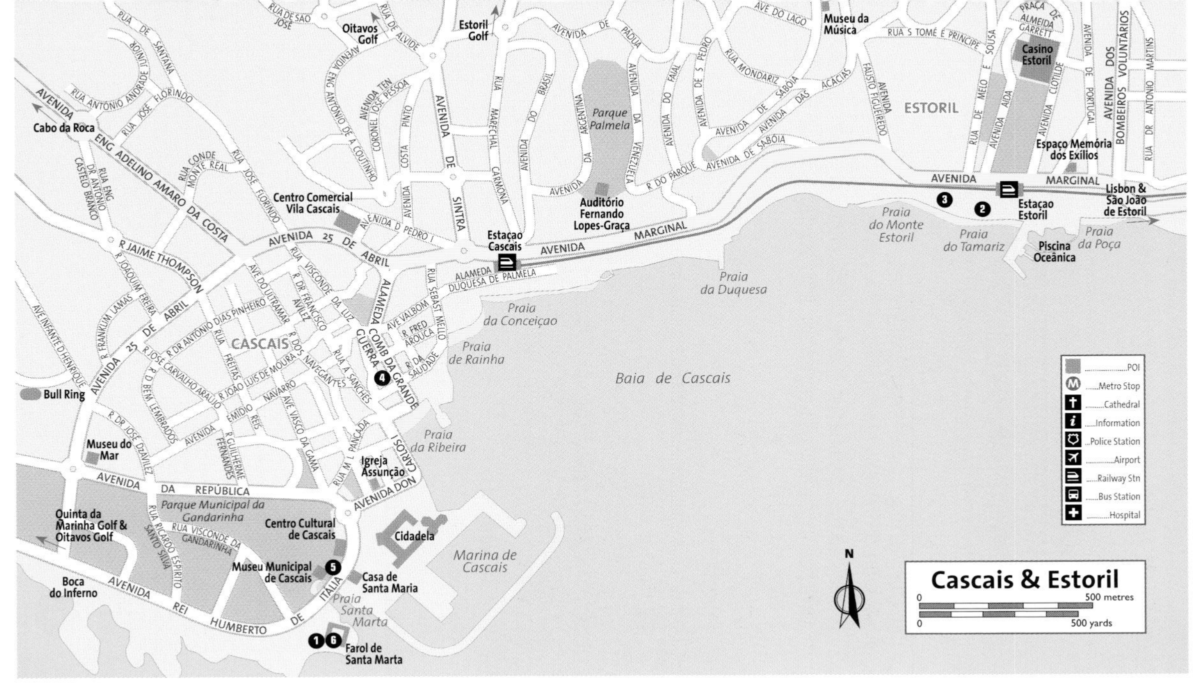
Cascais & Estoril
0 500 metres
0 500 yards
POI
Metro Stop
Cathedral
Information
Police Station
Airport
Railway Stn
Bus Station
Hospital
N
Baia de Cascais
CASCAIS
ESTORIL
Cabo da Roca
Oitavos Golf
Estoril Golf
Museu da Música
Casino Estoril
Espaço Memória dos Exílios
Lisbon & São João de Estoril
Estaçao Estoril
Estaçao Cascais
Parque Palmela
Auditório Fernando Lopes-Graça
Centro Comercial Vila Cascais
Praia do Monte Estoril
Praia do Tamariz
Piscina Oceânica
Praia da Poça
Praia da Duquesa
Praia da Conceiçao
Praia de Rainha
Praia da Ribeira
Bull Ring
Museu do Mar
Igreja Assunção
Parque Municipal da Gandarinha
Quinta da Marinha Golf & Oitavos Golf
Centro Cultural de Cascais
Cidadela
Marina de Cascais
Museu Municipal de Cascais
Casa de Santa Maria
Praia Santa Marta
Farol de Santa Marta
Boca do Inferno
AVENIDA MARGINAL
AVENIDA 25 DE ABRIL
AVENIDA ENG ADELINO AMARO DA COSTA
AVENIDA DE SINTRA
AVENIDA DA REPÚBLICA
AVENIDA REI HUMBERTO DE ITALIA
AVENIDA DON CARLOS I
ALAMEDA COMB DA GRANDE GUERRA
ALAMEDA DUQUESA DE PALMELA
R JAIME THOMPSON
RUA MARECHAL CARMONA
AVENIDA DA VENEZUELA
AVENIDA DA ARGENTINA
AVENIDA DE PADUA
AVENIDA DO BRASIL
RUA VISCONDE DA LUZ
RUA FREITAS
AVE VASCO DA GAMA
AVE DO ULTRAMAR
AVE INFANTE D HENRIQUE
AVENIDA DOS BOMBEIROS VOLUNTÁRIOS
AVENIDA DE PORTUGAL
RUA DR ANTÓNIO MARTINS
RUA S TOMÉ E PRINCIPE
AVENIDA FAUSTO FIGUEIREDO
AVE DO LAGO
RUA MONDARIZ
AVENIDA DE SABÓIA
AVENIDA DAS ACÁCIAS
AVENIDA DE S PEDRO
AVENIDA DO FAIAL
R DO PARQUE
RUA DE MELO E SOUSA
AVENIDA AIDA
AVENIDA CLOTILDE
PRAÇA DE ALMEIDA GARRETT
RUA DE ALVIDE
RUA DE SÃO JOSÉ
RUA DE SANTANA
RUA JOSÉ FLORINDO
RUA ANTÓNIO ANDRADE JUNIOR
RUA CONDE MONTE REAL
RUA ENG DR ANTÓNIO CASTELO BRANCO
AVENIDA ENG ANTÓNIO DE A COUTINHO
AVENIDA TEN CORONEL JOSÉ PESSOA
AVENIDA COSTA PINTO
AVENIDA D PEDRO I
RUA SEBAST MELLO
AVE VALBOM
R FRED AROUCA
R DA SAUDADE
R JOAQUIM ERERA
R FRANKLIM LAMAS
R DR ANTÓNIO DIAS PINHEIRO
R DR FRANCISCO AVILEZ
R DOS NAVEGANTES
RUA A SANCHES
R JOSÉ CARVALHO ARAUJO
R JOÃO LUIS DE MOURA
NAVARRO
AVENIDA EMÍDIO REIS
R GUILHERME FERNANDES
R D BEM LEMBRADOS
R DR JOSÉ DAVILEZ
RUA M L PANCADA
RUA VISCONDE DA GANDARINHA
RUA RICARDO ESPIRITO SANTO SILVA

SIGHTS & ATTRACTIONS

Boca do Inferno (Mouth of Hell)

This is a 150-million-year-old cavern with steep sides and deep gouges made by the turbulent sea. When it is windy and the sea is quite choppy, it is quite a spectacular sight to see the Boca turn into a mass of bubbling white water. You can reach it by walking west along the coastal road, but be careful of going too close, as some people have been swept away. ⓐ Av. Rei de Italia, Cascais Ⓝ Train: Cascais

Cabo da Roca

West of Cascais, and connected by regular buses (it's about 20 minutes away), this is the most westerly point in continental Europe. As well as containing a lighthouse, tourist office and other facilities, this is a great spot for walks and wild and dramatic views. ⓐ Cabo da Roca, Azóia

Casa de Santa Maria

Built by architect Raúl Lino in the early 20th century, this is a romantic combination of Mediterranean mansion and Moorish revivalist style. Look out for the 17th-century *azulejos* taken from an old chapel – which depict some quite horrific scenes – the elaborate ceilings and the view from the patio. ⓐ Estrada do Farol de Santa Marta, Marina de Cascais ⓣ (21) 481 5382 ⓛ 10.00–13.00, 14.00–17.00 Tues–Sun, closed Mon Ⓝ Train: Cascais

Casino Estoril

The largest casino in Europe, this has a theatre-auditorium, restaurants, art gallery and shops, as well as gaming rooms. It is strictly smart

Boca do Inferno is just outside Cascais

dress only (men with a jacket and tie). Praça José Teodoro dos Santos (21) 466 7700 www.casino-estoril.pt 15.00–03.00 Train: Estoril

Espaço Memória dos Exílios (Estoril Post Office Museum)

This is a modernist building designed by Portuguese architect Adelino Nunes and opened in 1942. As Estoril was a haven for many exiles during World War II, the first floor of the post office now has a permanent exhibition on this theme. Av. Marginal 7152A (21) 481 5930 10.00–18.00 Mon–Fri, closed Sat & Sun Train: Estoril

Igreja de Nossa Senhora da Assunção

Built in the 16th century, this church includes gilt-work on the wooden altar, panels of *azulejos* and the 17th-century paintings of the Annunciation by Josefa de Obidos. ⓐ Largo da Assunção ◷ 09.00–13.00, 17.00–20.00 ⓝ Train: Cascais

Marina de Cascais

Cascais Marina is a hub of social and sporting activity. Modern and well equipped, it has 650 moorings for boats as well as commercial space. Sailing races and regattas regularly start from here, and the sailing school **Escola de Vela Tuttamania** (ⓦ www.tuttamania.com) runs courses. The races are run by the **Clube Naval de Cascais** (ⓦ www.cncascais.com). There are also a few shops, restaurants and cafés surrounding the marina. ⓣ (21) 482 4857 ⓦ www.marinacascais.pt ◷ 09.00–18.00 (winter); 09.00–19.00 (summer) ⓝ Train: Cascais

Museu do Mar (Museum of the Sea)

Here you can discover the town's links with the sea and learn something about natural history and underwater archaeology. One of the most interesting parts of the museum includes models of boats and treasure salvaged from shipwrecks found off the coast. ⓐ Rua Júlio Pereira de Melo, Cascais ⓣ (21) 481 5906 ◷ 10.00–17.00 Tues–Sun, closed Mon ⓝ Train: Cascais. Admission charge

Museu Municipal de Cascais/Palácio dos Condes de Castro Guimarães

Housed in the 20th-century former mansion home of Jorge O'Neill, this place has fabulous ocean views. Sold to the Condes de Castro Guimarães in 1910, it underwent some alterations and today reflects the owner's penchant for acquiring art and furniture from various eras, including a neo-Gothic organ. The count died in 1927 and left

The marina at Cascais

the house to the local authorities, who turned it into a museum. Officially opened in 1931, there is a rich collection of *azulejos*, porcelain, furniture and a fine library of historic books. Av. Rei Humberto II de Itália, Parque Marechal Carmona (21) 482 5401 10.00–17.00 Tues–Sun, closed Mon Train: Cascais. Admission charge (except Sun)

ESTORIL COAST BEACHES

Most beaches along the Estoril Coast have been awarded a blue flag, in recognition of the water quality as well as the nearby infrastructure.

There are beaches and a promenade all the way from Cascais to Estoril. Praia da Ribeira by Cascais old town is a focal point because of the fishing boats that arrive here and the craft stalls and music performances, but it is not really a place to go swimming. Conceição, Rainha and Duquesa are small sandy beaches where you can hire sunbeds and grab a drink at one of the nearby bars. In Estoril the beaches include Monte Estoril, by the **Mirage Cascais Hotel** (ⓐ Av. Marginal 8554 ⓣ (21) 006 0600 ⓦ www.cascaismiragem.com), and Tamariz, which is popular with children, as there are pools of seawater. Further east is Poça, a calm and pleasant long beach, but the biggest stretch of sand and best place for watersports is Carcavelos near Oeiras. Popular with surfers, particularly in spring and autumn, it has volleyball and beach football pitches and a roller-skating rink. All have nearby cafés and restaurants.

For something a little more remote, you will have to drive west to Cabo da Roca (see page 122), then head north to Guincho. Naturally wild, it has a large area of sand dunes, long stretches of sand, and, because of the Atlantic wind, is good for surfing, body boarding and windsurfing.

Parque Municipal da Gandarinha

This large, leafy park stretches from the Condes de Castro Guimarães Museum to the Boca do Inferno. It is a pleasant place

Take a stroll along the promenade at Estoril

for a leisurely walk, faces the seafront and is filled with statues, ponds and palms, as well as the Cascais Sports Pavilion and the Manuel Passolo riding school. Av. Rei Humberto II de Itália Train: Cascais

CULTURE

Auditório Fernando Lopes-Graça

Named after one of the 20th century's famous Portuguese composers, this open-air auditorium is used for orchestral concerts, jazz, theatre and *fado* groups. ⓐ Parque Palmela, Avenida Marginal ⓣ (21) 482 5447 Ⓣ Train: Cascais

Centro Cultural de Cascais

Located on the site of a former 17th-century convent, the buildings were rebuilt by architect Jorge Silva as an art museum and exhibition centre. There is also an auditorium here, which is used for concerts. ⓐ Av. Rei Humberto II de Itália ⓣ (21) 484 8900 ⓑ 10.00–18.00 Tues–Sun, closed Mon Ⓣ Train: Cascais

Museu da Música/Casa Verdades de Faria (Music Museum/ Verdades de Faria House)

Wealthy arts patron Mantero Belard left this house to the town as a house-museum and gardens, and dedicated it to his mother. Decorated with painted stucco, glass and 17th-century tiles, today it houses a collection of Portuguese instruments bought from the Corsican ethnomusicologist Michel Giacometti. ⓐ Av. de Sabóia 1146B, Estoril ⓣ (21) 481 5901 ⓑ 10.00–13.00, 14.00–17.00 Tues–Sun, closed Mon Ⓣ Train: Estoril

RETAIL THERAPY

There are craft stalls on the beaches, traditional shopping in Cascais old town, and a weekly market next to the bullring, where you can find good-quality leather goods and jewellery. There is an open-air crafts fair during July and August by Casino Estoril, selling crafts from all over the country, including ceramics, tiles and woodcarvings.

There is a large shopping centre, **Cascais Shopping** (ⓦ www.cascaishopping.pt), located out of town towards Sintra on the EN9 road. You can catch buses 406, 417 and 418 from Cascais Station.

AFTER DARK

Cascais and Estoril have a good range of cafés and restaurants – many with outdoor seating areas – from traditional Portuguese tavernas to international cuisine. Watch out for touristy prices; there are reasonable places to be found. In Largo Luiz de Camões and Rua Frederico Arouca there are several bars and a few *fado* clubs. There are also a lot of bars around Cascais Marina, and Carcavelos Beach is also a popular choice.

RESTAURANTS

Coconuts Club £ ❶ A restaurant/club that's noted as much for its delicious, local-style nibbles as it is for its DJs and dancing. ⓐ Av. Rei Humberto II de Itália ⓣ (21) 484 4109 ⓦ www.nuts-club.com ⓛ 23.30–05.00 Tues–Sat (summer); Fri & Sat only (winter)

Jonas Bar £ ❷ Located on the edge of Tamariz Beach, this is a fast-food restaurant-bar where you can have burgers for lunch or stop for a beachfront drink in the evening. ⓐ Paredão, Praia do Tamariz ⓣ (21) 467 6946 ⓛ 08.00–02.00 May–Sept; 08.00–18.00 Oct–Apr

Restaurante Praia do Tamariz £ ❸ This beachside Spanish restaurant is good for tapas and paella. ⓐ Praia do Tamariz ⓣ (21) 468 1010

ⓦ www.restaurantepraiatamariz.com ⓛ 09.00–17.00 (winter); 09.00–02.00 (summer)

Restaurante Cervejaria Luzmar ££ ❹ A typical Portuguese surf 'n' turf restaurant where you should also try the seafood rice option (*arroz de marisco*). ⓐ Alameda dos Combatentes Grande Guerra 104 ⓣ (21) 484 5704 ⓦ www.luzmar.dcsa.pt ⓛ 12.30–16.30, 19.00–00.00 Tues–Sun, closed Mon

Restaurante Rosa Maria £££ ❺ This restaurant located inside the Farol Design Hotel serves good traditional Portuguese cuisine and has excellent sea views. ⓐ Av. Rei Humberto II de Itália 7 ⓣ (21) 482 3490 ⓛ 12.30–15.30, 19.30–23.30

ACCOMMODATION

Being a coastal resort area, the Estoril coast has no shortage of accommodation. For more options try ⓦ www.secretplaces.com & ⓦ www.estorilcoast-tourism.com

Clube do Lago £ This hotel in Monte Estoril offers apartment-style units with kitchenettes and has a well-equipped health club on the premises. ⓐ Av. do Lago 4 ⓣ (21) 464 7597 ⓦ www.hotelclubedolago.com ⓝ Train: Estoril

Estalagem Muchaxo £ Located on Guincho Beach, just a short distance from Cascais and Estoril, this is a typical Portuguese hotel with restaurant, breakfast room, bars, anti-stress centre, sauna and seawater pool. ⓐ Estrada do Guincho ⓣ (21) 487 0221 ⓦ www.muchaxo.com ⓝ Train: Cascais

Farol Design Hotel ££ This boutique hotel combines a 19th-century mansion with 21st-century interior design. It is located next to the marina and it has restaurants, bars and a saltwater swimming pool. ⓐ Av. Rei Humberto II de Itália 7 ⓣ (21) 482 3490 ⓦ www.farol.com.pt Ⓝ Train: Cascais

Hotel Cidadela ££ Just 500 m (1,640 ft) from the beach, this modern hotel has a bar, restaurant, swimming pool, poolside bar and barbecue. ⓐ Av. 25 de Abril ⓣ (21) 482 7600 ⓦ www.hotelcidadela.com Ⓝ Train: Cascais

Hotel Estoril Eden ££ A large hotel with guest rooms and apartments, it also has an indoor and outdoor swimming pool, jacuzzi, sauna, massage service, sunbeds, restaurant and poolside snack bar. ⓐ Av. de Sabóia 209 ⓣ (21) 466 7600 ⓦ www.hotel-estoril-eden.pt Ⓝ Train: Estoril

Hotel Inglaterra ££ This grand Estoril hotel in a converted mansion has a great location near the beach and steps from the Casino. ⓐ Rua do Porto 1 ⓣ (21) 468 4461 ⓦ www.hotelinglaterra.com.pt Ⓝ Train: Estoril

Hotel Albatroz £££ Situated on the bay, this is one of Portugal's top boutique hotels. A privately owned residence, each of its rooms has a unique character. ⓐ Rua Frederico Arouca 100 ⓣ (21) 484 7380 ⓦ www.albatrozhotels.com Ⓝ Train: Cascais

Hotel Quinta da Marinha £££ Perched on the cliff tops facing the sea and with views of the Sintra hills, this resort hotel has two pools, golf course, tennis courts, restaurants and bars. ⓐ Quinta da Marinha ⓣ (21) 486 0100 ⓦ www.quintadamarinha.com Ⓝ Train: Cascais

Sintra

Sintra is great to see if you have more than a couple of days in the Lisbon area. Surrounded by the green and rocky hills of the Serra da Sintra, its palaces, castle, houses and museums are among the country's top attractions. A UNESCO Heritage Site since 1995, the Romans, Moors and Portuguese royal family all adored it here, and with the advent of the Lisbon–Sintra railway in the 19th century it became a summer resort for the middle classes. You can easily walk around the Vila Velha (historic centre), dominated by the Palácio Nacional, but it is easier to take a bus or car to see the Palácio da Pena and some of the other attractions.

Each year Sintra hosts one of the most famous music festivals in the country, and the Centro Cultural Olga Cadaval (see page 138) hosts a string of exciting concerts and performances.

Getting around Sintra is easy – a bus (434) runs every 20 minutes from the train station to the historic centre and the Palácio Nacional, the Castelo dos Mouros, Palácio da Pena and back to the station. A rover ticket allows you to hop on and off where you please. Alternatively you can ride in one of the horse-drawn carriages that operate between Sintra and the Serra – you will see these in front of the Palácio Nacional.

Sintra's local authority website covers all aspects of tourism and culture in the area. Ⓦ www.cm-sintra.pt

GETTING THERE

Rossio Station in Lisbon is the most central station for reaching Sintra; trains run regularly (every ten minutes) and the journey only takes 40 minutes. There are also trains from the Oriente and

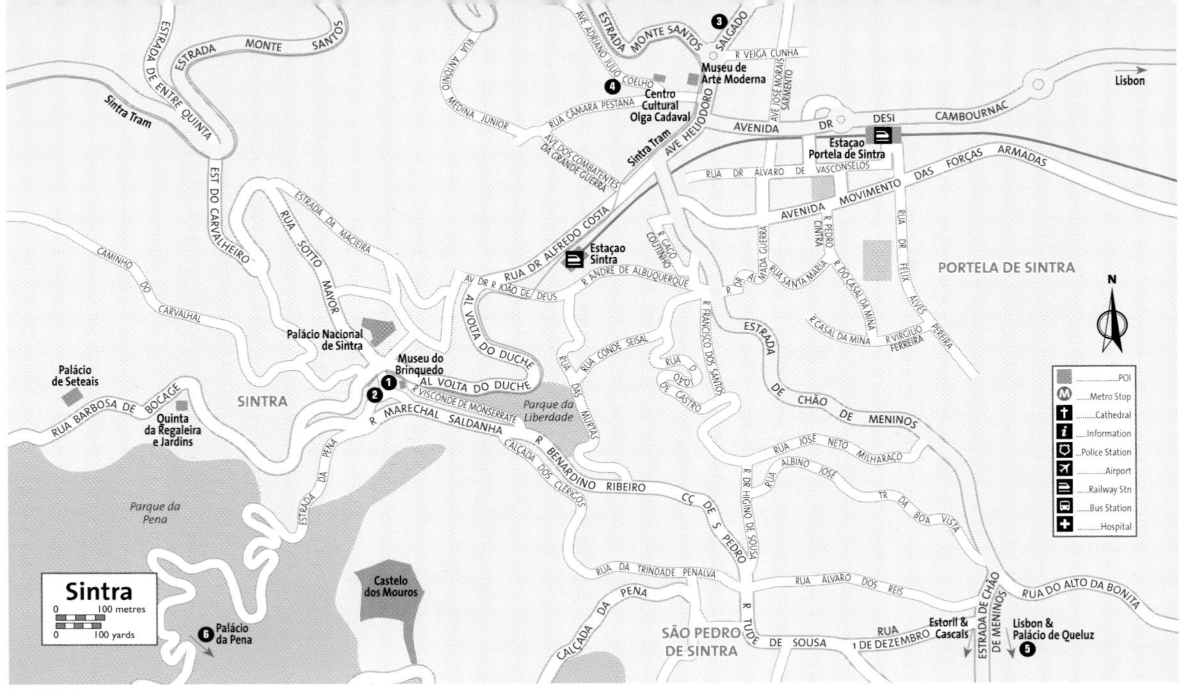

Sintra
0 100 metres
0 100 yards
N
POI
Metro Stop
Cathedral
Information
Police Station
Airport
Railway Stn
Bus Station
Hospital
Lisbon
PORTELA DE SINTRA
SINTRA
SÃO PEDRO DE SINTRA
Estaçao Portela de Sintra
Estaçao Sintra
Museu de Arte Moderna
Centro Cultural Olga Cadaval
Palácio Nacional de Sintra
Museu do Brinquedo
Palácio de Seteais
Quinta da Regaleira e Jardins
Parque da Liberdade
Parque da Pena
Castelo dos Mouros
Palácio da Pena
Estoril & Cascais
Lisbon & Palácio de Queluz
Sintra Tram
ESTRADA MONTE SANTOS
ESTRADA DE ENTRE QUINTA
EST DO CARVALHEIRO
CAMINHO DO CARVALHAL
RUA BARBOSA DE BOCAGE
ESTRADA DA MACIEIRA
RUA SOTTO MAYOR
RUA ANTÓNIO MEDINA JUNIOR
AVE ADRIANO JULIO COELHO
RUA CAMARA PESTANA
AVE DOS COMBATENTES DA GRANDE GUERRA
AVE HELIODORO SALGADO
R VEIGA CUNHA
AVE JOSÉ MORAIS SARMENTO
AVENIDA DR DESI CAMBOURNAC
RUA DR ALVARO DE VASCONSELOS
AVENIDA MOVIMENTO DAS FORÇAS ARMADAS
RUA DR ALFREDO COSTA
AV DR R JOÃO DE DEUS
AL VOLTA DO DUCHE
R GAGO COUTINHO
R ANDRÉ DE ALBUQUERQUE
R DR AL MADA GUERRA
RUA SANTA MARIA
R PEDRO CINTRA
R DO CASAL DA MINA
R CASAL DA MINA
R VIRGILIO FERREIRA
RUA DR FELIX ALVES PEREIRA
R FRANCISCO DOS SANTOS
ESTRADA DE CHÃO DE MENINOS
RUA D JOÃO DE CASTRO
RUA CONDE SEISAL
RUA DAS MURTAS
R VISCONDE DE MONSERRATE
R MARECHAL SALDANHA
R BENARDINO RIBEIRO
CÇ DE S PEDRO
CALÇADA DOS CLÉRIGOS
ESTRADA DA PENA
RUA JOSÉ NETO MILHARAÇO
RUA ALBINO JOSÉ
TR DA BOA VISTA
R DR HIGINO DE SOUSA
RUA DA TRINDADE PENALVA
RUA ALVARO DOS REIS
CALÇADA DA PENA
R TUDE DE SOUSA
RUA 1 DE DEZEMBRO
ESTRADA DE CHÃO DE MENINOS
RUA DO ALTO DA BONITA

Entrecampos stations which stop at Queluz on the way to Sintra. Trains leave every half hour and take 75 minutes from Oriente to Sintra; 39 minutes from Entrecampos.

SIGHTS & ATTRACTIONS

Castelo dos Mouros (Moorish Castle)

Originally built by the Moors around the 8th and 9th centuries in dramatic surroundings on two hills in the Serra de Sintra, the castle was conquered by Dom Afonso Henriques in the 12th century and rebuilt by Dom Fernando in the 19th century, when the walls were

Sintra's Castelo dos Mouros is a worthy reminder of Moorish style

PALÁCIO NACIONAL DE QUELUZ (QUELUZ NATIONAL PALACE)

This pink palace is located between Lisbon and Sintra, so you might like to stop off for a tour. It is often referred to as a 'little Versailles' for its elegance and formal gardens filled with baroque statues. Today the East Wing is the official residence of foreign dignitaries invited by the Portuguese state. Highlights include the façade of the palace, the Music Room, the Throne Room, the collection of Portuguese furniture and the gardens. ⓐ Largo do Palácio de Queluz ⓣ (21) 434 3860 ⓛ Palace: 09.30–17.00 Wed–Mon, closed Tues; gardens: 10.00–18.00 (summer), 10.00–17.00 (winter) Wed–Mon, closed Tues ⓡ Train: Queluz. Admission charge

restored. The walls and turrets of the castle can be seen winding their way around the ridges of the hills. Look out for the chapel built by Dom Afonso with its Romanesque doorways, tracings of paintings and medieval tombs, as well as the Moorish cistern and the 'royal tower'. ⓐ Rua da Pena ⓣ (21) 923 7300 ⓛ 09.00–19.00 1 May–14 June; 09.00–20.00 15 June–15 Sept; 09.00–19.00 16 Sept–31 Oct; 09.30–18.00 1 Nov–30 Apr ⓡ Train: Sintra; Bus: 434 from Sintra. Admission charge

The impressive Parque da Pena is a 200-hectare (494 acres) garden surrounding the palace.

Palácio Nacional de Sintra (Sintra National Palace)

As you approach Sintra, look out for the unmistakeable white chimneys of the National Palace, also known as the Paço Real or Palácio da Vila.

A mixture of mudejar (Arabic-style), Gothic, Manueline and Renaissance styles, it is a national monument.

You cannot fail to admire the stunning mudejar *azulejos* that cover the walls of various halls, patios and the royal chapel. Renaissance style was added during the reign of Dom João III (1521–57), who built the Sala dos Cisnes, where you can see various royal portraits. The Sala dos Brasões contains 18th-century tiles by the best masters of the time. ⓐ Largo Rainha Dona Amélia ⓣ (21) 910 6840 ◷ 10.00–17.30 Thur–Tues, closed Wed ⓦ Train: Sintra; Bus: 434 from Sintra

Palácio da Pena (Pena Palace)

Located in the Serra da Sintra on the peak of a rocky hill, this 19th-century palace was built on the orders of Dom Fernando II. The former monastery had been severely damaged by the 1755 earthquake, but around the remaining Renaissance altar of the chapel, a palace of Moorish, Gothic, Manueline and Renaissance pastiche was built, influenced by the European castles of the time. Don't miss the original 16th-century Manueline cloisters, the odd-shaped sentry boxes, the 18th-century tiles, period furniture and the murals, as well as impressive views across the park and surrounding area. ⓐ Estrada da Pena ⓣ (21) 910 5340 ◷ 10.00–17.30 (summer); 10.00–16.30 (winter) ⓦ Train: Sintra; Bus: 434 from Sintra. Admission charge

Quinta da Regaleira e Jardins (Regaleira Estate & Gardens)

This fascinating palace and gardens are worth a visit if you are interested in mystery, mythology and fantasy. It is a beautiful combination of architectural styles, built at the beginning of the 20th century. Look out for the neo-Gothic, neo-Manueline carved stone motifs, the labyrinthine gardens, statues, grottoes, waterfalls

You can't miss the unmistakeable chimneys of the Palácio Nacional in Sintra

and lakes, as well as the dry well with the Templar's cross, eight-pointed star and a chapel. Underneath is a crypt that leads into a gallery connecting it to the palace. You can visit the palace and gardens, but if you want a guided visit you should book ahead.

ⓐ Rua Barbosa du Bocage ⓣ (21) 910 6650 ⓛ 10.00–17.30 Nov–Jan; 10.00–18.30 Feb, Mar & Oct; 10.00–19.00 Apr–Sept ⓝ Train: Sintra; Bus: 434 from Sintra. Admission charge

Sintra tram

Hop on this tram for a relaxing ride to the wine-growing town of Banzão, near Colares, and on to Praia das Maças, where you will find the best-known beach on the Sintra coastline. The tram is near the Museu de Arte Moderna in Sintra. ⓣ (21) 923 8789 ⓛ Fri–Sun (summer only): first tram leaves Sintra at 10.00, last tram leaves Praia das Maças at 16.45

CULTURE

Centro Cultural Olga Cadaval

This cultural centre was restored and updated after it was damaged by fire in 1985. Today it hosts concerts, theatre and performing arts events. ⓐ Largo Dr Vergilio Horta ⓣ (21) 910 7100 ⓦ www.ccolgacadaval.pt ⓛ 14.00–18.00 Mon–Fri, 10.00–13.00, 14.00–18.00 Sat, closed Sun; booking office closes one hour before event starts ⓝ Train: Sintra; Bus: 434 from Sintra

Museu de Arte Moderna (Museum of Modern Art)

This museum is a treat for 20th-century art lovers. It houses an interesting collection of European and American art. The Berardo Collection, as it is known, includes works by Pablo Picasso, Miró, Max Ernst, Man Ray, George Segal, Andy Warhol and Roy Lichtenstein. ⓐ Av. Heliodoro Salgado ⓣ (21) 924 8170 ⓦ www.berardocollection.com ⓛ 10.00–18.00 Wed–Sun, 14.00–18.00 Tues, closed Mon ⓝ Train: Sintra; Bus: 434 from Sintra

One of many interesting exhibits from the toy museum

Museu do Brinquedo (Toy Museum)
Here you can see the toy collection of João Arbués Moreira, gathered together over the course of 50 years, from teddy bears and carousels to soldiers and Dinky toys. Rua Visconde de Monserrate (21) 910 6016 www.museu-do-brinquedo.pt 10.00–18.00 Tues–Sun, closed Mon Train: Sintra; Bus: 434 from Sintra

RETAIL THERAPY

Don't expect large state-of-the art shopping centres in the middle of Sintra. Wander the tangle of streets of the Vila Velha and you are bound to find some treasures, from local crafts, traditional instruments and antiques to books, pottery and wine. The **Loja do Arco** (Rua Arco do Teixeira 2) is a treasure trove of Portuguese music, from *fado* to classical and contemporary, as well as books and sheet music. It also has internet access. For hand-painted Portuguese ceramics try

Sintra Bazar and A Esquina (both in Praça da República), head to **Almorábida** (ⓐ Rua Visconde de Monserrate 12–15) for lace, and **Casa Branca** (ⓐ Rua Consiglieri Pedroso 12) for linens and embroidered silks.

TAKING A BREAK

There are several cafés in the Old Town area, including by the station and tram, in case you have to wait. While in Sintra you should try a *queijada*, a tasty local cake made from cheese, eggs, sugar, flour and cinnamon.

A Piriquita £ ❶ Great for pastries. ⓐ Rua das Padarias 1–5, off Rua Visconde de Monserrate ⓣ (21) 923 0626 ⓛ 09.00–22.00

Enjoy outdoor dining at a restaurant in Sintra

Vila Velha £ ❷ Good for a quick snack. Stop by for a salad, sandwich or *caldo verde*. It is located along the narrow alleyway opposite the Palácio Nacional. ⓐ Rua das Padarias 8, off Rua Visconde de Monserrate ⓣ (21) 923 0154 ⓛ 08.00–19.00

AFTER DARK

RESTAURANTS & BARS

Tirol de Sintra £ ❸ A good basic place for lunch or dinner, this restaurant has outdoor seating and serves traditional Portuguese cuisine. Specialities include roast leg of lamb, pork meat with clams, pizzas, home-made breads and *queijada*. ⓐ Av. Heliodoro Salgado 5 ⓣ (21) 923 0505 ⓛ 07.00–20.30

Casa Orixás ££ ❹ This Brazilian restaurant has a choice of buffet or à la carte menu with food from various regions, as well as tropical gardens and lively ambience. ⓐ Av. Adriano Julio Coelho 7 ⓣ (21) 924 1672 ⓦ www.orixasclub.com ⓛ 16.00–00.00 Tues–Thur, until 01.00 Fri, 11.00–01.00 Sat, until 00.00 Sun, closed Mon

Cozinha Velha £££ ❺ Located in the former palace kitchen at the Palácio Nacional de Queluz (see page 135), this superb restaurant offers fine dining in luxurious surroundings. ⓐ Largo do Palácio ⓣ (21) 435 6158 ⓛ 12.30–15.00, 19.30–22.00

Restaurante Palácio Nacional da Pena £££ ❻ You can dine on traditional Portuguese cuisine at the restaurant inside the Palácio Nacional, but you will pay for the pleasure. ⓐ Estrada da Pena ⓣ (21) 923 1208 ⓛ 12.00–16.00, 19.00–22.00

ACCOMMODATION

Casal da Carregueira ££ Small guest house set in enclosed gardens near Queluz, dressed in period furniture with a bar, comfortable sitting room, sauna and barbecue area. ⓐ Belas ⓣ (21) 432 1474 ⓦ www.portugalvirtual.pt Train: Sintra

Hotel Tivoli Sintra ££ Located in the centre of Sintra, this hotel has a bar and restaurant with panoramic views of the valley. ⓐ Praça da República ⓣ (21) 923 7200 ⓦ www.tivolihotels.com Train: Sintra

Quinta de São Thiago ££ On the lower slopes of the Sintra hills, this 16th-century house has been modernised but has retained its chapel, old tiles, library and music room. There is also a swimming pool and tennis court. ⓐ Estrada de Monserrate ⓣ (21) 923 2923 ⓦ www.portugalvirtual.pt Train: Sintra

Penha Longa Hotel & Golf Resort £££ Large resort hotel with three restaurants, beautiful gardens, two golf courses, spa, health club, indoor and outdoor pools, tennis courts and a jogging track. ⓐ Estrada da Lagoa Azul, Linhó ⓣ (21) 924 9011 ⓦ www.penhalonga.com Train: Sintra

Pousada de Queluz – Dona Maria I £££ Located by Queluz National Palace, 5 km (3 miles) from Lisbon. Comfortable rooms with mini-bar and satellite TV. ⓐ Largo do Palácio ⓣ (21) 435 6158 ⓦ www.pousadas.pt Train: Queluz-Belas

◐ *An underground train pulls in at Chelas Station*

PRACTICAL
information

Directory

GETTING THERE

By air

Several airlines currently operate from the UK to Aeroporto da Portela, Lisbon's international airport. Schedules are liable to constant change, so do check the websites of the following carriers while planning your journey:

Air Berlin ⓣ 0871 500 0737 ⓦ www.airberlin.com
British Airways ⓣ 0870 850 9850 ⓦ www.ba.com
easyJet ⓣ 0800 612 7279 ⓦ www.easyjet.co.uk
Monarch ⓣ 0870 040 5040 ⓦ www.flymonarch.com
TAP Portugal ⓣ 0845 601 0932 ⓦ www.flytap.com

From North America, TAP Portugal (see above) and **Continental** (ⓦ www.continental.com) are the only airlines that offer non-stop flights from New York. Most major US airlines offer flights, but with a change of planes somewhere in Europe.

From Australia, British Airways (see above) offers flights via London. Most other airlines, like **Qantas** (ⓦ www.qantas.com.au) and **Cathay Pacific** (ⓦ www.cathaypacific.com), fly to Lisbon but with a stopover somewhere in Asia (like Singapore or Hong Kong) and in Europe. From New Zealand, **United Airlines** (ⓦ www.united.com) offers flights via Los Angeles and London.

Many people are aware that air travel emits CO_2, which contributes to climate change. You may be interested in the possibility of lessening the environmental impact of your flight through the charity Climate Care, which offsets your CO_2 by funding environmental projects around the world. Visit ⓦ www.climatecare.org

By rail

To reach Lisbon by rail you will have to be prepared for a long haul and a few changes, but this might be an option if you are buying a multi-country train pass with stops along the way. From London you can take one of the frequent Eurostar services to Paris Gare du Nord station. From there you should transfer to Paris Montparnasse or Austerlitz and take a train to Hendaye/Irún. Overnight trains run direct from here to Gare do Oriente (see page 48). It takes at least 24 hours to do the journey non-stop. See www.railpass.com or call 0844 848 4064 for exact connections and tickets.

Eurostar 0870 518 6186 www.eurostar.com

SNCF (France) www.voyages-sncf.com

ENTRY FORMALITIES

Citizens of EU countries can enter Portugal with either a valid identity card or passport. Citizens of Canada, the United States, Australia and New Zealand must travel with their passport but do not need a visa if staying for less than 90 days. Citizens of South Africa require a visa.

Travellers to Portugal are currently entitled to bring the following duty-paid goods into the country for their own personal use: up to 800 cigarettes, 10 litres of spirits, 90 litres of wine (60 litres of sparkling wine), and 110 litres of beer. However, if you are questioned by Customs officials and cannot satisfy them that it is not for commercial use, it could be seized and not returned.

If you are travelling to and from non-EU countries, you still have a duty-free allowance of 200 cigarettes or 50 cigars or 250 g of tobacco; two litres of wine or one litre of spirits; plus 50 g of perfume, 250 ml of *eau de toilette* and gifts worth up to 50 euros.

MONEY

Portugal adopted the euro in 2002, and its former currency, the escudo, was withdrawn from circulation. Euro notes are available in denominations of 5, 10, 20, 50, 100, 200 and 500 euros; coins are available in 1, 2, 5, 10, 20 and 50 cents plus 1 and 2 euros. One side of the coin is common throughout the EU but the flipside is individual to the country where it was minted. However, all currency can be used throughout the EU countries where the euro is used.

You can change money and traveller's cheques, but be prepared to pay a commission – traveller's cheques should be in US dollars, pounds sterling or euros. However, with so many ATMs around, it is more likely that you will prefer to withdraw money as and when you need it. Most cards are accepted and the instructions are multilingual. Credit cards are also accepted at most places.

HEALTH, SAFETY & CRIME

Citizens of the EU are entitled to reduced-cost and sometimes free medical treatment on production of a European Health Insurance Card (EHIC). You can apply for this on-line from the UK Department of Health (W www.dh.gov.uk). The card lasts for three to five years and covers medical treatment in the case of emergency or accident. Also make sure you take identification with you as well as your EHIC. As this may not cover all your medical needs it is better to have your own private travel insurance to pay for repatriation, should you need it. Insurance also usually covers you if you are a victim of crime, but check your policy carefully before you travel.

Although Lisbon does not have a high crime rate compared with some cities, there has been a rise in violent crime in the past couple of decades. In general, Lisbon is safe, but tourists are easy targets for opportunists. Watch out for pickpockets in crowded areas, particularly where there is a high concentration of tourists, such as on tram no. 28 (see page 56). Be careful when travelling back to your hotel late at night, especially in the dark, narrow streets of the Alfama, Bairro Alto and Chiado. If you are unlucky enough to be the victim of a crime, contact the tourist police in Praça dos Restauradores (☎ (21) 342 1634). For lost property, ask the tourist police where you can find the nearest *Guardia Nacional da República* (GNR, National Guard).

OPENING HOURS

Most shops tend to open from 09.00–13.00 and 15.00–19.00 Mon–Fri. On Saturday some shops only open from 09.00–13.00. However, the large shopping centres are open from 09.00–00.00. Banking hours are generally 08.30–15.00 Mon–Fri, but some branches in Lisbon reopen from 18.00–23.00. Most museums open from 10.00–18.00 Tues–Sun, but this can vary – some also close for lunch.

TOILETS

There are public toilets in shopping centres, department stores such as El Corte Inglés, and most museums. There are also toilets in the main railway stations. Cafés and bars have toilets but it is always better and more polite to buy something first.

CHILDREN

Most Portuguese are very good with children, and families regularly go out together to eat in the evening, even late at night. Children are welcome in most places except late-night bars and clubs. Depending on the age of the children, some museums and historic attractions might not be exciting enough for them. They might like to climb up the towers of the Castelo de São Jorge (see page 74), the Torre de Belém (see page 101) and ride on the trams and elevadors.

Parque das Nações (see page 110) has various suitable attractions, including the Pavilhão do Conhecimento (see page 112), the Oceanário (see page 110), and the Teleférico (see page 112).

At **Lisboa Zoo** (ⓐ Estrada de Benfica ⓣ (21) 723 2900 ⓦ www.zoolisboa.pt) there is a wide range of animals, from big cats and camels to tropical birds and reptiles. Feeding time is a good time to take the children, and there are numerous rides as well. There are various activities for children in the Parque Florestal de Monsanto (see page 88), and the beaches of the Estoril coastline are also close enough to take a day trip. They are easily reached by train from Cais do Sodré.

You can hire bicycles in the Parque das Nações – there are many safe routes here, and **Tejo Bike** (ⓐ Rossio dos Olivais or Sony Plaza ⓣ (21) 891 9333 ⓦ www.tejobike.pt) is a most reliable outfit. There is a discount of 20 per cent if you have a Parque das Nações Card (see page 113). If you do go for the card, you'll also be able to use the Tourist Mini Train to travel round the Parque das Nações. The route begins and ends at Alameda dos Oceanos in front of the Pavilhão Atlântico.

COMMUNICATIONS

Internet

Internet cafés include:

Lisbon Welcome Centre ⓐ Praça do Comércio ⓣ (21) 031 2810 ⓛ 09.00–20.00

Net Centre Café ⓐ Rua Diário de Noticias ⓛ 16.00–02.00

Peter Café Sport ⓐ Rua da Pimenta, Parque das Nações ⓛ 11.00–01.00

Phone

Many people prefer to take their mobile phones abroad these days rather than use a public phone. Before you go remember to contact

Belém Tower is right on the River Tagus

your mobile provider to make sure your phone is activated for international use. Also check that your existing handset will work in Portugal and ask how much the charges for calls and texts will be. You will often have to pay for receiving calls while abroad and texts can be charged twice, depending on the provider. Phone providers in Portugal include **Vodafone** (www.vodaphone.com) and **Optimus** (www.optimus.pt).

TELEPHONING PORTUGAL

To call Portugal from abroad, dial the international access code (00), then the country code (351), then the phone number (including the provincial/area code, which, for Lisbon, is 21), omitting the initial zero.

TELEPHONING ABROAD

To call abroad, dial 00, then the country code and city/local code, minus the first 0, then the phone number you require. You can also make calls at post offices and pay for the call at the end. The country code for the UK is 44, for Ireland 353, for the USA and Canada 1, for Australia 61, for New Zealand 64 and for South Africa 27.

Telephones in hotels are also convenient but tend to be quite expensive for anything other than a local call. A list of charges should be provided in your room. If they aren't, ask at reception.

Using a public telephone box is quite easy, and direct dialling in Lisbon is not a problem. Public phones can be found in cafés and bars as well as stations and in the street. Phones take euro coins in denominations of 2 cents up to 2 euros. Alternatively, phone cards can be bought from newspaper kiosks, the post office or other retail outlets – ask for a CrediPhone – and they come in units of 50, 100 or 150.

The garish Palácio da Pena in Sintra

Post

Post office (*correios* ⓦ www.ctt.pt) opening times can vary in the larger cities. The main post offices in Lisbon, Cascais, Estoril and Sintra can be found at:

ⓐ Praça dos Restauradores, Lisbon ⓛ 08.00–22.00

ⓐ Aeroporto, Lisbon ⓛ 24 hours

ⓐ Avenida Marginal, Lote C, Cascais ⓛ 09.00–18.00

ⓐ Avenida Nice 1, Estoril ⓛ 09.30–19.30

ⓐ Praça Don Afonso Henriques 7 ⓛ 08.30–18.00

ELECTRICITY

Voltage is 220 volts using standard continental Europe two-pin sockets. To use American appliances, a 220-volt transformer should be used, together with an adapter plug.

TRAVELLERS WITH DISABILITIES

Lisbon's cobbled streets and hilly geography make it rather a challenge for wheelchair users or anyone with a physical disability. However, access for travellers with disabilities is improving gradually and some hotels now offer adapted rooms and bathrooms. Modern buildings are generally fairly accessible, but wherever you go it is a good idea to call in advance and be clear about your needs.

For general advice on accessible travel contact:

RADAR The principal UK forum for people with disabilities. ⓐ 12 City Forum, 250 City Road, London EC1V 8AF ⓣ (020) 7250 3222 ⓦ www.radar.org.uk

SATH (Society for Accessible Travel & Hospitality) advises US-based travellers with disabilities. ⓐ 347 Fifth Ave, Suite 605, New York, NY 10016 ⓣ (212) 447 7284 ⓦ www.sath.org

TOURIST INFORMATION

There are three main tourist offices in Lisbon:
Airport (21) 841 3700 08.00–00.00. Located in the main arrivals hall, use this kiosk to ask for immediate information on accommodation, maps and main attractions. You also need to go here to pick up a taxi voucher into the city centre.
Palácio Foz, Praça dos Restauradores (21) 346 3314 09.00–20.00. You can pick up information here. and there is also a shop.
Praça do Comércio (21) 346 3314 09.00–20.00. This is the main tourist office, the Lisbon Welcome Centre, and provides detailed information on accommodation, attractions, tours, discount cards and travel cards. It also has a café, internet access and a shop.

Lisbon's tourist office website covers both the city as well as Estoril, Leiria/Fatima, Costa Azul, Sintra, Templarios, Oeste, Ribatejo and other places close by. www.atl-turismolisboa.pt

The Lisbon local authority website also has a good tourist information section. www.cm-lisboa.pt

BACKGROUND READING

Lisbon by Paul Buck. An interesting insight into the city. A cultural and literary companion, the book provides factual information on the city's history and sights, often through the views of artists and writers.
The Last Kabbalist of Lisbon by Richard Zimmler. A crime thriller set in the 16th century, during the time of Jewish persecution.

Emergencies

For police, ambulance and fire services, the number is 112

MEDICAL SERVICES

In an emergency you should go to the nearest public hospital, which will provide emergency treatment. EU citizens with a European Health Insurance Card (see page 146) are entitled to reduced-cost, and sometimes free, basic treatment. Medical insurance is advisable for EU citizens and essential if you are a non-EU visitor.

If you can get to a hospital yourself, head for *urgências* or a 24-hour public health clinic. *Farmacia* (pharmacies) can help you with a list of emergency clinics, doctors and dentists.

British Hospital Rua Tomás da Fonseca (21) 721 3400

Clinica Internacional de Saúde de Cascais Rua João Infante, Lote 1 r/c A, Alto das Flores, Bairro do Rosario, Cascais (21) 486 5946 www.cis-cascais.pt

Hospital Santa Maria Av. Prof Egas Moniz (21) 780 5000; Urgencias: (21) 780 5111 and (21) 780 5222 www.hsm.min-saude.pt

Doctors

Dr David Ernst Clínica Médica Internacional de Lisboa, Av. António Augusto Aguiar (21) 351 3310

Dr Andrew French International Health Centre, Rua do Regimento Dezanove 67, 2nd floor (21) 484 5318

Dentists

Dr Francis Haley B.D.S. and Dr D B Skinner Av. 25 de Abril, Edificio Grei 184, 1st floor, Cascais (21) 486 3011

POLICE

The tourist police are located in Praça dos Restauradores (ⓣ (21) 342 1634).

EMBASSIES & CONSULATES

Australian Embassy ⓐ Av. da Liberdade 200, 2nd floor ⓣ (21) 310 1500 ⓦ www.portugal.embassy.gov.au

Canadian Embassy ⓐ Av. da Liberdade 198–200, 3rd floor ⓣ (21) 316 4600 ⓦ www.portugal.gc.ca

Irish Embassy ⓐ Rua Imprensa-Estrela 1, 4th floor ⓣ (21) 392 9440

New Zealand Consulate ⓐ Rua do Periquito, Cascais ⓣ (21) 370 5779

South African Embassy ⓐ Av. Luís Bívar 10 ⓣ (21) 319 2200 ⓦ www.embaixada-africadosul.pt

UK Embassy ⓐ Rua de São Bernardo 33, Lisbon ⓣ (21) 392 40 00 ⓦ www.uk-embassy.pt

US Embassy ⓐ Av. das Forças Armadas ⓣ (21) 727 3300 ⓦ lisbon.usembassy.gov

EMERGENCY PHRASES

Help!	**Fire!**	**Stop!**
Socorro!	Fogo!	Pare!
Sookohrroo!	*Fohgoo!*	*Pahreh!*

Call an ambulance/a doctor/the police/the fire brigade!
Chame uma ambulância/um médico/a polícia/os bombeiros!
Shami ooma angboolangsya/oong medeekoo/a pooleesseeya/ oosh bombehroosh!

WHAT'S IN YOUR GUIDEBOOK?

Independent authors Impartial up-to-date information from our travel experts who meticulously source local knowledge.

Experience Thomas Cook's 165 years in the travel industry and guidebook publishing enriches every word with expertise you can trust.

Travel know-how Contributions by thousands of staff around the globe, each one living and breathing travel.

Editors Travel-publishing professionals, pulling everything together to craft a perfect blend of words, pictures, maps and design.

You, the traveller We deliver a practical, no-nonsense approach to information, geared to how you really use it.